Prai
The Idealist.o
Building a

"*The Idealist.org Handbook to Building a Better World* helps idealists of all ages assess and identify their interests and motivations, and provides the tools, strategies, and inspiration to become engaged and active citizens."

> —Jon McConnell, Associate Director for Public Service Education, Haas Center for Public Service, Stanford University

"Archimedes, the Greek mathematician, said, 'Give me a lever and a place to stand and I'll move the world.' This book is a timely primer on what our own lever might look like, and where we should put it if we wish to change the world. Given the explosion of interest in trying to make a difference—through offering time, talent, or treasure—this book provides compelling, easy-to-follow guidance on how to turn good intentions into effective world-changing actions."

> —Kevin F.F. Quigley, President, National Peace Corps Association

"At once practical and inspirational, this book asks the simple but penetrating questions: Are you an idealist? If so, what are you going to do about it? A must-read for anyone interested in making a difference, changing their life and community—in short, building a better world."

> —Patrick Corvington, Senior Associate, The Annie E. Casey Foundation

"This has to be the single best book for those who want to translate good intentions into action. It clearly presents the myriad ways in which each of us, regardless of our age, resources, or preferences, can have a positive impact on our community. Whoever you are, whatever you are doing, this book will empower you to help make this world a better place. A must-read for idealists everywhere!"

> —Bill Alberta, Associate Director, Cornell Career Services

continued...

"This book provides invaluable advice by helping readers reflect upon their dreams for building a better world then find ways to turn those good intentions into action. Its tone is refreshingly non-ideological, non-preachy, and just plain practical. I would highly recommend this book to individuals of all ages, as well as to university and community libraries."

—Bill Nolting, Assistant Director of Education Abroad,
University of Michigan International Center

"The concept for this book is so heartwarming. It tugs at, tempts, and thrills the idealist in all of us. With so many examples of ways to invest time, talent, and dollars, it underscores the idea that anyone can help make the world a better place. As with any good guidebook, you will find yourself marking it up and referring to it often."

—Linda Wiener, Aging and Workforce Consultant,
Wiener Training and Consulting Group

"Idealist.org's website has been a powerhouse of information and knowledge for more than a decade, and this new book captures and shares those resources with anyone who has ever hoped to 'make a difference.' Not only do the explanations make the nonprofit sector accessible, but the emphasis on using solid career-education tools, such as self-assessment, research, and networking, ensures identifying and finding a perfect fit for using one's skills, time, or resources to build a better world. This book should prevent the idealist in anyone from becoming a pessimistic realist."

—Beth Olson, Associate Director, Center for Career Education,
Columbia University

"Idealist has taken another step toward removing the barriers between bright ideas and good actions, empowering people of all ages and talents to contribute toward building that better world."

—Lynne Schuman, Director of Career Services and
Alumni Affairs, Humphrey Institute of Public Affairs,
University of Minnesota

"From donating money to exploring corporate social responsibility, this resource will engage all who want to create a better world. It goes beyond other volunteer resources by discussing ways to contribute in nonprofit and for-profit organizations, in the workplace as well as through volunteering. The creative suggestions for involvement offer a fresh look at civic engagement."
>—Andrea Smith Shappell, Assistant Director, Center for
>Social Concerns, University of Notre Dame

"An absolute must-have for any college career adviser! This book provides the needed tools to enable students and alums to explore options in nonprofit from volunteering to making career changes. The in-depth materials in this book provide keen insight into motivation, self-knowledge, organizations, resources, and much more. This is a much-needed resource."
>—Greg Hatch, Assistant Director, The Career Center,
>University of Illinois

"*The Idealist.org Handbook to Building a Better World* offers an often overlooked message that you can contribute to the nonprofit world in many ways beyond direct service. There is great information about how to contribute your time, expertise, or money through volunteering, board service, and philanthropy, whether you work at a for-profit or nonprofit organization. This book conveys its message in an inspiring, no-nonsense style and provides a concrete roadmap to help you move from good intentions to actions. I highly recommend it."
>—Joseph Du Pont, Esq., Director, Hiatt Career Center,
>Brandeis University

"*The Idealist.org Handbook to Building a Better World* shows us how to make a difference in unconventional ways. It opens the reader's mind to overlooked talents and forgotten passions and inspires action. The most empowering message from the experts at Idealist.org is that building a better world through taking action is possible, no matter how small that action may be. This is a provocative yet practical guide for readers to uncover their passions and skills and use them to make a difference, not only for others but also for themselves."
>—Linda Arra, Director, Career Services, Lafayette College

continued...

"For anyone who wants to make a positive difference in the world, I can hardly think of a more excellent resource. This book is a very practical guide to putting one's desire to help others into action. Whether through gifts of time, talent, or treasure, this marvelous work provides a roadmap for taking concrete steps toward enhancing the lives of others."

—Jim Lindsay, Executive Director, Catholic Network of Volunteer Service

"Designed for those looking to make positive contributions to society, this book leads individuals through a process of self-assessment by encouraging them to think about the issues that matter most to them, as well as their experience, skills, and limitations. Filled with valuable resources, this is perfect for the individual who has always wanted to give back but never knew where to start. Start by reading this book!"

—Rebecca Zirm, Director of Recruitment, Mandel Center for Nonprofit Organizations

"For those who find themselves asking the question, 'How can I make a difference in my community?' *The Idealist.org Handbook to Building a Better World* is an excellent place to discover some answers. This is the best resource for living a life of action that makes a difference. I know of no other resource that packs so much practical information for those who seek to contribute to the common good."

—Scott Hudgins, Assistant Dean, The Graduate School, University of North Carolina at Greensboro

"*The Idealist.org Handbook to Building a Better World* is an outstanding resource for anyone who wants to make a difference but is not sure how to begin. This down-to-earth, highly informative book is useful both to beginning job seekers and experienced professionals considering a career change. I highly recommend this book."

—Dee Thompson, Director, Career Center, Portland State University

The Idealist.org Handbook to Building a Better World

How to Turn Your Good Intentions into Actions that Make a Difference

Idealist.org with Stephanie Land

A PERIGEE BOOK

A PERIGEE BOOK
Published by the Penguin Group
Penguin Group (USA) Inc.
375 Hudson Street, New York, New York 10014, USA
Penguin Group (Canada), 90 Eglinton Avenue East, Suite 700, Toronto, Ontario M4P 2Y3, Canada
(a division of Pearson Penguin Canada Inc.)
Penguin Books Ltd., 80 Strand, London WC2R 0RL, England
Penguin Group Ireland, 25 St. Stephen's Green, Dublin 2, Ireland (a division of Penguin Books Ltd.)
Penguin Group (Australia), 250 Camberwell Road, Camberwell, Victoria 3124, Australia
(a division of Pearson Australia Group Pty. Ltd.)
Penguin Books India Pvt. Ltd., 11 Community Centre, Panchsheel Park, New Delhi—110 017, India
Penguin Group (NZ), 67 Apollo Drive, Rosedale, North Shore 0632, New Zealand
(a division of Pearson New Zealand Ltd.)
Penguin Books (South Africa) (Pty.) Ltd., 24 Sturdee Avenue, Rosebank, Johannesburg 2196,
South Africa

Penguin Books Ltd., Registered Offices: 80 Strand, London WC2R 0RL, England

While the authors have made every effort to provide accurate telephone numbers and Internet
addresses at the time of publication, neither the publisher nor the authors assume any responsibility
for errors, or for changes that occur after publication. Further, the publisher does not have any
control over and does not assume any responsibility for author or third-party websites or their
content. The organizations, companies, and websites cited by the authors are for informational
purposes only and, as such, are not endorsed in any way by the authors or the publisher.

First edition: March 2009

Library of Congress Cataloging-in-Publication Data

The Idealist.org handbook to building a better world : how to turn your good intentions into
actions that make a difference / Idealist.org with Stephanie Land.— 1st ed.
  p.   cm.
Includes bibliographical references and index.
ISBN 978-0-399-53487-4
1. Volunteerism. 2. Social service. 3. Idealism. 4. Idealist.org. I. Land, Stephanie.
HN49.V64I34 2009
361.3'7—dc22   2008047913

PRINTED IN THE UNITED STATES OF AMERICA

10   9   8   7   6   5   4   3   2   1

PUBLISHER'S NOTE: This publication is designed to provide accurate and authoritative
information in regard to the subject matter covered. It is sold with the understanding that the
publisher is not engaged in rendering legal, accounting, or other professional services. If you require
legal advice or other expert assistance, you should seek the services of a competent professional.

Contents

Part III. Idealism at Work

Acknowledgments

This book could not have been written without the many people who took the time to share their experience, knowledge, and stories with us. These generous people include: Caroline Altman Smith, Lois Blevins, Laura Bonsett, Matt Davis, Pat DiGeorge, Jackee Engles, Rena Feretti, Charlotte Frank, Justin Ho, Matt Holton, James Jones, Valerie Jones, Ken Kagle, Cliff Landesman, Kim Lowery, Susan MacEachron, Christine Millen, Kathy Moreland, David Murphy, Greg Nelson, Jessica Newman, Lucy Stroock, Chris Tebben, Janet Thompson, Betsy Werley, Linda White, and Alynn Woodson.

Thanks to the committed staff at Idealist.org who provided support and research for this project, particularly Meg Busse, Jung Fitzpatrick, Chris Machuca, Steven Pascal, and Amy Potthast.

Additional appreciation is due the following people, who spent considerable time refining chapters related to their expertise: Erin Barnhart (Volunteering), Putnam Barber (Philanthropy and Nonprofit Basics), and Jake Brewer (Socially Responsible Business).

A big thank-you to Maria Gagliano, our editor at Penguin, for her guidance, her patience, and her belief in this book.

I don't know how to begin to share my appreciation of the hard work of our coauthor, Stephanie Land. She listened, asked good questions, distilled information from many sources, and was a great partner in every way.

This book is the product of the Idealist.org staff's collective effort to help people move from good intentions to action. I have had the good fortune to work with Lorene Straka and Ami Dar in achieving these goals for nine years and fourteen years, respectively. Aside from their feedback in editing this book, they also inspire and challenge me every day to do my best work.

My interest in doing good was inspired in large part by the example set by my parents, Brenda and Leonard Finkelstein. In the process of working on this book I was able to rely even more on Patrick Hickey, who does good work daily and makes me want to be better.

Finally, thank you to all those who we at Idealist meet every day through our work. It is your desire to do more that keeps us going.

Russ Finkelstein
Associate Director, Idealist.org

Preface

Do you remember yourself as an eight-year-old? I was born in Israel, but I grew up in Mexico City, and I have a very clear memory from an evening there in my seventh or eighth year. We were driving somewhere, it was raining hard, and my sister and I sat in the back of the car and looked out the window.

My father stopped at a red light, and as often happened then, a young boy came up to the car to ask for some money. Because it was dark and raining, I didn't see him until he was right next to us, with his hands against my window and his face only a few inches from mine. We looked at each other for a moment, I could see that he was about my age, and then the light changed and we drove away.

What I remember most strongly, apart from his eyes looking at me through the rain, was asking my parents: Why? Why is he out there while we are in here? What can we do? How can we help?

That feeling of wanting to do something, anything, stayed with me, and years later it led me to start Idealist.org as a place where anyone could find a way to turn those questions into actions.

Idealist is now almost fourteen years old, and in this book we want to take everything we have learned through our work and share it with you. Our hope is that through the tips and ideas we've collected here, you will find your own way to answer these questions.

As a great example of turning intentions into action, this book would not exist without the idealism, the creativity, and the stubbornness of our associate director, Russ Finkelstein. He picked it up when it was just an idea and ran with it until it was done. Russ, thank you!

Ami Dar
Founder and Executive Director, Idealist.org

Introduction

Why did you pick up this book? Are you a recent graduate with dreams of a career that directly relates to your passions and interests? Are you successfully engaged in a lucrative job and eager to apply your professional skills and resources toward a greater cause? Are you approaching retirement but not ready to spend your days on the proverbial golf course? Or are you just tired of running around in the hamster wheel of daily routine?

If any of these scenarios sound familiar, you've come to the right place.

The Idealist.org Handbook to Building a Better World was written for people like you—people seeking a greater sense of fulfillment, connection, and purpose, people eager to reach out and make a difference beyond the confines of their cubicle or dorm or living room. It is for people who dream big yet appreciate how little it takes to make a difference, people who have decided they do not want to stand on the sidelines when there's so much to be done to make the world a better place.

This book will reveal the countless surprising ways in

which you can change the world and show you how to find the opportunity that fits perfectly with your needs and aspirations. Regardless of how you want to (or can) get involved, the information in these pages will provide you with the tools and resources you need to jump off that hamster wheel and turn all your good intentions into action.

WHO WE ARE

Since 1995, Idealist.org has been trying to make the world a better and more connected place. We maintain a family of websites and we organize events for individuals and organizations—mostly nonprofits—eager to make an impact at local, national, and global levels, serving as a hub where people and organizations can come together. Without Idealist.org, these groups might otherwise never find one another. Though our formal mission statement is "to help build a world where everyone can live free and dignified lives," you could say that our informal mission is to do away with missed opportunities—the opportunity to share ideas, information, and resources, and to participate in an endless range of projects, services, and organizations. Thus, a school in Nepal can connect with talented English teachers interested in traveling abroad; a Washington, DC, rape crisis center can find its newest intern—a local high school student with dreams of becoming a domestic abuse lawyer; a graphic designer with an interest in consumer protection issues can find and partner with a writer in Los Angeles who is thinking of starting a newsletter on the subject; the project manager at a computer software company can learn of a school whose playground needs to be rebuilt, and mobilize her colleagues to pitch in. The way we see it, anyone with an urge to help should easily be able to find a group or an individual who could benefit from their time, talent, money, or professional expertise.

This was the challenge our executive director, Ami Dar, grappled with for years before starting Idealist.org. A lifelong news junkie, Ami was inspired by the idealism of the people he'd meet during his travels. Everywhere he went—on trains in Peru, in youth hostels in Europe, on hiking trails in Chile—there were bright, energetic people itching to change the world, and many of them had smart, innovative ideas on how to do it. What if there were a way to bring those ideas together and make the most of this deep, global pool of talent, goodwill, resources, technology, and time?

In 1993 that way became clear when someone came to Ami's apartment and introduced him to the Internet. And so Idealist.org was born. For the first few years, the organization consisted of Ami, his first hire Russ (now associate director), and a few staffers housed in an office loaned to us by a generous company, Aladdin Knowledge Systems, in New York City.

Now with more than a million members in two hundred countries, offices in New York City; Portland, Oregon; and Buenos Aires; and staff members in Geneva; Berlin; Seattle; San Francisco; and Appleton, Wisconsin, Idealist.org is a do-gooder nerve center, acting as a literal idea list and a virtual bulletin board for people eager to get involved and organizations who want to find them and reach out to them. Each day we provide people with free job, internship, and volunteer opportunities, and inform them of events around the world that might match with their interests. We are the only global nonprofit information site that cuts across issues—we don't limit ourselves to any cause, country, or creed. We also provide a comprehensive, one-stop source for all your questions about nonprofits, how they work, who works for and with them, and the challenges and advances they face. In addition, we convene people locally, facilitating nonprofit career, graduate school, and global volunteer fairs throughout the United States and Canada, as well as organizing opportunities for local people to meet others who want to improve their communities, from Afghanistan to Zambia. In short, there's something for everyone. You can see a full list of our resources in the Resources section at the end of this book.

HOW TO USE THIS BOOK

Aside from schools or church groups, the most popular and often easiest route along which most nascent idealists begin their journey is by getting involved with a nonprofit, and it is in making those successful connections between people and organizations that our expertise lies. Yet while this guide contains all the information you need to understand the nonprofit world, we're not going to overwhelm you with the nuts and bolts of nonprofit organizational strategy. We're more interested in offering an overall look at the myriad opportunities the nonprofit world provides, and giving you a chance to do some soul searching and tap into that which will give you a sense of fulfillment.

Yet nonprofits are by no means the only way through which people can channel their good intentions. You can spearhead your own projects and fund-raisers, or choose to work for a socially responsible business, or simply harness the resources available at your workplace. We're going to explore the pros and cons of all of these options, too. There is no right way to put your good intentions into action. What matters is simply that you do. We recognize that people change and that life takes us down paths we never imagined. What fulfills you now is not necessarily what will fulfill you later; what you have to give now may change in the future. Although we have written this book to address the needs of anyone hoping to get involved in changing the world, not every chapter will be relevant to your current circumstances. You may use the book to research volunteer opportunities today, but keep it on hand because next year you may decide you're ready to join a board. It is our hope that this book will become a familiar reference for you whenever your needs change.

Part I covers nonprofit basics, such as how organizations work and why they are a primary avenue through which people with energy and passion can have a tremendous impact on a cause or community. We'll encourage you to think in broad terms about what issues you find most important and how to let your values and beliefs guide your decision about how and where to contribute your time, money, or skills. We strongly recommend that everyone read this section, since the more you understand about how nonprofits function, the better equipped you'll be to hit the ground running no matter how you get involved with one.

We will also lead you through a personal exploration of your particular skills, gifts, and talents to help you ascertain exactly what you have—and what you want—to offer. And we'll review the various roles available to you within nonprofits depending upon your expertise in a given area and the level at which you want to get involved.

Part II will tell you everything you need to know about the three most effective ways to contribute your time, expertise, or money: volunteering, board service, and philanthropy. As you'll see, there are many more ways to serve your community or have an impact on the world than you may imagine. In these chapters you'll read about many worthy nonprofits tackling all kinds of issues. We have included these examples to give you an idea of the variety of nonprofits that exist, but we hope you won't limit yourself to the ones you find in this book. Our goal is not to promote one organization over another, and there are far too many out there for us to include all those that are doing great work. There is, however, an organization out there that is a perfect fit for you. So don't settle for the ones we tell you about. Rather, use our suggestions as a springboard from which to embark on your own explorations.

Lastly, Part III will specifically address the needs and concerns of individuals working in the for-profit world who are eager to put to greater use the resources available to them. We'll show you what changes you can initiate from within your current workplace, and that making a difference doesn't require making a huge financial contribution or having a PR department (though we'll also show you how to leverage these should they be an option). We'll discuss the potential upsides for seeking out hybrid or for-benefit companies, businesses formed with the dual mission of making a profit and promoting a social good. In Chapter 9, we'll examine corporate social responsibility—what it is, why it's important, how it will influence us, what it promises for our future.

Part III will also provide guidelines for those people who have decided to make the transition from their current job in a for-profit to a nonprofit or "for-benefit" career. The best news? Contrary to what your parents or professional mentors might have told you, you can make a good living while doing good. We'll provide important information about how to prepare professionally, psychologically, and financially before taking this leap.

WHY THIS BOOK

The Idealist.org Handbook to Building a Better World is about much more than getting a job in the nonprofit sector or finding a volunteer opportunity. It's about empowerment. No matter where you are in life—student, professional, stay-at-home parent, retiree—you already have everything you need to make an impact, to make your voice heard, to make the changes you think need to be made. This book will help you connect the dots. We should tell you up front that we don't care what it is you want to do. We don't have any agenda about where you spend your money or which political party you align yourself with. All we care about is helping you find a way to connect with other people and groups who care about the same things you do.

So whether you identify yourself as conservative, liberal, or something in between, what you really are is an idealist. You believe in the value and importance of certain principles or policies or goals; you believe they are worth promoting and protecting; you believe in the power of one, and you believe in the power of working together. We want to help you harness that power. Whatever your goals, we salute you for getting involved. Now, let's get started.

PART I

An Idealist Is Born

1

I Want to Help, Where Do I Start?

So you want to make a difference. You can start by congratulating yourself; just by picking up this book, you've taken a huge step. A lot of people talk about "getting involved," but they never manage to turn their good intentions into action. To many, it can seem tough to fit do-gooding into a busy life. But taking your place among the tens of millions of idealists already acting to make a difference really isn't that hard.

One thing we believe strongly at Idealist.org is that there is a way for everyone to make the world a better place. Too many people are under the impression that the only way to show they care about an issue is by volunteering a set number of hours each week with a nonprofit organization or donating money. That's just not the case. There is no standard by which caring or compassion or generosity can be measured—at different times you'll have different resources to offer, and different issues that energize and move you. It's all up to you and what you decide you have to give. As you think about where and how you'd most like to make a difference, keep in mind that whatever you choose, you're not necessarily making a lifetime commitment. Gone are the days when a company hired you with the expectation that you'd work for them for thirty-five years. The same goes for nonprofits and other organizations that have made it their mission to serve or advocate for the good of a community or cause. They are generally eager to form new relationships.

All you need to do is decide where you fit in, and what will work best for you. Figuring that out is the focus of this chapter.

CONSIDER THE OPTIONS

Doing good feels pretty good. Take it from these idealists:

> "At the core, I believe volunteering is essential to my reason for being alive and present at this place and time."

> "You literally get a little chemical high when making a donation. I think it's a great chance to put your values into action."

> "I have learned more about what it truly means to be wealthy [by working for a nonprofit] than I ever could have working for a for-profit."

> "During my MBA we had a professor from Cameroon talk about the use of technology in developing countries. This was the first time I had come across the concept of the digital divide, and when I heard about it I thought, 'Yes!—this

is my niche, this is how I can transfer my skills from the corporate sector to a nonprofit.'"

"Of course I could still tutor or serve a meal, but I decided the greatest impact I could have on an issue I care about was to take on the challenge of being a board member. Somehow it just feels like this is the way to show true commitment not just to an issue, but to this organization."

Each of these people contributes in vastly different ways to his or her respective organization, whether by volunteering, donating money, working on staff, providing pro bono professional skills, or serving on a board, and each approach is equally valuable in supporting a nonprofit's efforts. There are three types of contribution, however, that anyone who bridges the gap between good intentions and effective action will make, alone or in various combinations. To begin thinking about how you'd like to make an impact, you first need to acknowledge which of these resources you most want to share and to which you have the most access: time, money, or expertise.

Time

We've established that one major reason people hesitate to act on their good intentions is that they don't know where to start. The other big reason people cite for not getting more involved in causes and organizations that mean something to them is lack of time. A lot of people are exhausted when work, parenting, or other pursuits suck up the greater part of the day, and they're unwilling to give up limited family time, or friend time, or couch potato time, no matter how much they admire and support the cause. And that's OK. Choosing downtime over service doesn't make a person selfish or uncaring.

Yet if you have few obligations after a day at the office, supporting a nonprofit after hours (whether paid or unpaid) is a great way to make a difference while still bringing in your steady paycheck. On the other hand, maybe you are working part-time and are looking for the perfect place to spend the other half of your day or week. Maybe your youngest child just started school or left for college. Maybe you're one of the seventy-six million baby boomers who at the time of this writing might be contemplating retirement. Or maybe you're dissatisfied with the job you've got now and excited by the idea of starting a brand-new career that allows you to devote your working hours to a cause that matters to you. In any of these cases, you've got time to give—sometimes a little, sometimes a lot—and you just need to figure out what to do with it.

The most obvious way to donate your time is to volunteer with a nonprofit. There are many reasons why people volunteer—religious convictions, altruism, class credit, networking, to make new friends, to get out of the house, even guilt…the list goes on and on. But there is really only one reason why people *continue* to volunteer: because they get something in return. That something might be a fresh group of contacts for your business, or some work experience to bolster your resume, or a chance to build some skills you need to earn a promotion at your for-profit job. But the biggest something, the biggest reason by far that most people give for why they volunteer is the feeling it gives them—of pride, of camaraderie, of fulfillment. It's a feeling that lasts long after the time has been spent. If it's true that time is money, donating time to a cause you care about rewards you with a pretty impressive return on your investment (ROI).

At the time of this printing, a quick browse on the Idealist .org website reveals more than fifteen thousand volunteer opportunities around the world, and that's only a small percentage of what's available out there. Narrowing our choices, we find that an organization in New Jersey needs child advocates for abused and neglected kids; a Boston nonprofit is looking for someone to help archive their documents and presentation materials; a tutoring service in Virginia has put a call out for individuals to help recent immigrants practice their English-language skills; an NGO (non-governmental organization) in Venezuela needs carpenters and construction workers on-site, as well as "virtual volunteers" who stay in their native countries and use the Internet to complete research, translation, and fund-raising projects. None of these four positions requires experience, and all of the organizations offer necessary training. Fifteen thousand volunteer opportunities. Perhaps you've got some time for one of them?

By the way, let's say you are one of those people who would rather spend their free time with their TiVo. We get it, really we do. Work/life balance is as important to us as it is to you. But you should know that contributing your time to a good cause doesn't have to be a daily thing, or even a weekly thing. The time commitment for the positions mentioned above range from two hours a week to twenty hours a month, but some describe it as "flexible" and the work can be done on-site or at home. You can change the world in an hour, a day, a year—the options are endless.

> **What has surprised me most about my volunteering experience is that I have somehow found the time to do it.**
>
> —Pat DiGeorge, volunteer, Rotary Club; Roswell, Georgia

It's important, too, to remember that you don't have to limit yourself to what the nonprofit asks of you or posts in their listing. There's no reason why you can't call or write to an agency and tell them that you've got an hour a week to spare, is there something you could do for them? We'll talk more later about ways in which you can be proactive in your volunteer service to ensure that it suits your needs and goals.

Whether you've got a little or a lot, any time you've got to offer is an extremely precious resource, one that many nonprofits would be delighted to put to great use. Think about how you'd like to spend it while we cover the other two types of contribution you might be able to make.

Money

Maybe the resource you have the most access to is money. After all, it often seems that the relationship between time and money is inversely proportional—the more we have of one, the less we have of the other. If you're an executive or ER surgeon or work-from-home parent, or that business you started has taken off beyond anything you could have imagined, it's possible you don't have one more hour in your life to donate to a worthy cause. But perhaps for the first time you have a little extra money. You've got your expenses covered, and you'd like to do something good with what's left over. Maybe you're ready to implement a corporate giving program at your company to help spread the wealth you've created. Alternatively, perhaps you're not swimming in dough, but you've decided that you can do with a little less so that others can have a little more.

> In 2006, 90 percent of U.S. adults said they had made financial contributions to a charity in the past twelve months, including 94 percent of people earning less than $35,000 per year.[1]

Many organizations rely upon knowing that every year they can count on a certain amount of dollars coming from a particular source, whether it's a consistently generous individual, many small donations from dues-paying members (such as AARP), a foundation, or a corporation. It is thanks to these continuous donations that nonprofits can plan ahead for the year and make sure that they've got their basic expenses covered while they also work on increasing their reach and improving their services.

There's no doubt that as an individual's or family's fortunes rise and fall, so does the amount they are willing or able to part with to support the work done by nonprofits.

In 2006, families with annual household incomes of less than $35 thousand gave a mean of $368. Families with household incomes between $35 and $49.9 thousand gave $721; between $50 and $74.9 thousand gave $926; and over $75 thousand gave $2,205.[2]

For our purposes we're going to stretch the definition of philanthropy. The reason is that at Idealist.org, we don't believe there's a difference in the intrinsic worth of large donations and small ones. Each one serves its purpose; each one is given by someone eager to make the world a better place. To us, everyone with this instinct deserves the title of philanthropist.

What's the emotional ROI of donating money versus donating time? For many people, it's the same. You've got to prioritize, and if family or work has to take precedence over service, that's OK. By writing a check you're doing your part to make the world a better place. Donating money to a nonprofit is by no means a lesser form of giving. Far from it. Most nonprofits cannot survive without donations, and that check you write can go a long way toward making sure they fulfill their mission. You can take great satisfaction in knowing that you've made their work possible.

And there's another ROI you can enjoy—the tax deduction. As long as you or your business are donating money to a nonprofit that qualifies as a 501(c)(3) organization, and you itemize your returns, Uncle Sam will reimburse a percentage of any money you give them. Everybody wins.

We'll define what makes a 501(c)(3) organization in Chapter 2.

Maybe our enthusiasm for the tax deduction that comes with making philanthropic or charitable donations surprises you. We're idealists, not ascetics. In the end, we don't care if you're giving out of a moral imperative and/or because it lowers your tax rate. In fact, it's common for people's motives for supporting charitable work to be mixed. Regardless of your reasons for donating, there's a nonprofit out there that's going to be able to do a lot of good with that money. All we care about is that you're happy with the choices you make and that you achieve fulfillment through your act of philanthropy, or any act of giving.

As with time, the amount of money you can or wish to donate is relatively unimportant. What is important is determining how much you can spare and where you'd like to see it put to use. Best of all, the only time donating takes is the time you want to spend researching organizations before allocating your money.

We'd like to reiterate here that it's not just about money, but about meaning, and we're referring to what your donation means to you, not the nonprofit. Just because you have money doesn't mean you should give it away. Sure, it's fantastic if you choose to give money to the soup kitchen so they can offer another five hundred meals on Thanksgiving. But if giving money doesn't give you the sense of connection you're after, maybe you'd like to consider volunteering to serve food to the hungry. Of course, there's no reason why you can't make both contributions if that's an option for you. But if it's not, or if you decide to do one and not the other, you shouldn't feel like you're not doing enough.

Expertise

Donating time or money are common ways of contributing to a good cause, but your expertise can also be an incredibly valuable resource to a nonprofit. Wait a minute, you might say, I'm an accountant, the artists' collaborative I've always wanted to work with can't do anything with me. (Yes, they can.) I'm a student, I don't have any expertise yet. (Sure you do.) You'd be surprised at the variety of ways in which a nonprofit can put your academic knowledge or professional experience or even just your street smarts to good use.

There are two influential roles people who want to contribute their expertise most commonly fill within a nonprofit.

Board Membership. The first is becoming a board member. Every independent nonprofit is supervised by a board—a group of individuals, usually voted in after an interview process, that handles the establishment of bylaws, fund-raising activities, and supervising the long-term needs of the organization. Joining a board is an excellent way for people with the resources of time and expertise—and sometimes money, but not always—to make a huge contribution to a cause they believe in.

Why not volunteer? You can. But some people like to

marry their skills to their service or infuse their career with some variety. Attorneys might enjoy drawing on their understanding of the law in a different setting than the courtroom; art historians might relish the opportunity to help develop and grow a young gallery's national reputation; grant writers might jump at the chance to use their skills to help launch a charter school. Board membership is a strategic role. Anyone can be a volunteer, which is part of the appeal of volunteering. But a board member, though also a volunteer, helps build strong, sustainable, long-term systems, resources, and relationships, and helps ensure the future of the organization. In Chapter 6 we'll explore how anyone, regardless of age, education, economic status, or profession, can become a board member, and go over the details of how boards work and what potential members need to know before joining.

Skilled Volunteering. As we've said, most volunteer positions require no previous experience. There is a way, however, to harness your professional experience to expand the amount of good you can do using the skills and knowledge you get paid to use every day. A cosmetologist, for example, might bring a lot of joy to the elderly if she were to donate a few hours a week to a senior citizens' center. A butcher could work with an organization that distributes venison donated by hunters to the hungry. Alternatively, some people work with a nonprofit specifically to get involved in something completely separate from their job; the last thing they want to do is more of what they do on a daily basis. They may, however, have a particular skill that they have developed out of passion. Skilled volunteerism is a great way to apply that skill for the good of an organization. For example, an engineer may also be an excellent photographer with a collection of top-grade equipment. That person could be a tremendous asset to an agency who needs someone to document their activities for their website and other media venues.

The challenge, unfortunately, is that nonprofits, like many organizations, aren't always good at thinking outside the box. If a nonprofit that builds homes for the needy knows you are an architect or construction manager, it may be hard to convince them to forgo those professional skills and instead take advantage of your writing skills for the newsletter. However, as far as we're concerned, there's no point in making any contribution if it's only going to become another chore for you to slog through. You've got enough of those. This is your opportunity to add something great to your life. For you to be able to sustain your best, most gratifying work for the longest period of time, you must be allowed to use the skills you choose in the environment of your choice. If you can't make a match between your needs and those of the organization, don't ever hesitate to tell them the same thing you would to a pleasant but uninspiring date—I like you, but this just isn't the right fit.

> There is one option you have with a nonprofit that you don't with a date: an open-ended rejection. It's perfectly OK to tell a nonprofit that they aren't the right fit for you—for now. You can add that you value the work of the organization and would be interested in serving in the future should the opportunity arise.

Getting the Most Out of Your Contribution

You'll notice that we talk a lot about the emotional and psychic benefits of contributing to a nonprofit you care about. Some people believe in the theory that service can't be about you, that if you're going to do it, you have to check your needs at the door. We disagree. People volunteer, serve on boards, or engage in skilled volunteering for a number of reasons, and we believe all of them are valid. For example:

Making a difference
Getting exercise
Giving back
Honing leadership skills
Getting to know a new community
Improving civic involvement
Enhancing your resume
Learning something new
Spending time outdoors
Accomplishing a new challenge
Building networks for the good of your business
Exploring new career options
Serving as a role model for your kids
Just for the fun of it

Many people who originally volunteer or donate funds for altruistic reasons are pleasantly surprised to find how many of these tangible benefits they take away from their term of service.

WHAT MATTERS TO YOU?

As your access to time, money, or expertise fluctuates, so will your contributions to whatever nonprofit(s) with which you decide to get involved. That's why it's always helpful to know why you got involved in the first place.

For most of us, including those who smile when they get that tax deduction, giving back to our community or working to change the world stems from a belief that a little individual effort from one can make a difference to another, and even many. Some people, on the other hand, seek to fill an emotional or spiritual void. Whatever your reasons, they're good ones, and it's important to think a little more about them as you decide how you want to participate in organizations devoted to service or advocacy.

In particular, there's a big question to think about, one which may sound a little clichéd but which is key to establishing where to begin your journey: What matters to you?

We realize it's a broad thing to ask, the kind of question that can send your mind spinning in a thousand different directions. And that's OK. This is not the time for self-censorship—the possibilities are endless and you should explore every avenue. Think about your interests, your passions, the things that drive you crazy or give you the biggest thrill. Do you make it your mission to find a home for every stray who pads into your backyard? Maybe you'll want to focus your efforts on animal rescue, or the zoo, or a group that trains Seeing Eye dogs. Find ways to pull together the things that you love. If you have a teaching background, perhaps you could bring animals into nursing homes and offer lectures about the history of certain breeds. Think about how to combine your interests and skills. Do you have a family member in a wheelchair? Perhaps you'd be compelled to join a foundation that supports families raising children with disabilities. Do you also love music? There are countless opportunities for musicians and audiophiles to share their knowledge and expertise. And what if you combined these interests and joined forces with a nonprofit that strives to make music venues more accessible to the disabled? Consider the role that you'd like to play in a nonprofit and use your passion and interests to create it.

The list below is a tiny sample of the thousands of organizations that address causes, issues, and problems toward which you could apply your skills and talent if you live in, say, Milwaukee, Wisconsin. There's no particular reason that we chose Milwaukee other than it's a medium-size city (that also happens to be home to the International Clown Hall of Fame, which is kind of cool).

DOMESTIC VIOLENCE

Caritas for Children

Daystar, Inc.

Kids Matter, Inc.

La Causa Crisis Nursery

Lutheran Social Services

Meta House

Milwaukee Women's Center

Sexual Assault Treatment Center

St. Rose Youth and Family Center, Inc.

Task Force on Family Violence, Inc.

Word of Hope Ministries, Inc.

ENVIRONMENT

Community Shares of Greater Milwaukee

Growing Power

Havenwoods State Forest

Keep Greater Milwaukee Beautiful

Milwaukee Habitat for Humanity

Milwaukee Public Museum

Pettit National Ice Center

Rebuilding Together Greater Milwaukee

Schlitz Audubon Nature Center

Urban Ecology Center

Wehr Nature Center

Zoological Society of Milwaukee

HEALTH

Alzheimer's Association SE WI Chapter

American Cancer Society

American Lung Association of Wisconsin

Arthritis Foundation—Wisconsin Chapter

Aurora Visiting Nurse Association of Wisconsin Hospice

Blood Center of Wisconsin, Inc.

Center for the Deaf and Hard of Hearing

CORE/El Centro

Easter Seals Kindcare Southeastern Wisconsin

Friedens Community Ministries

Gilda's Club Southeastern Wisconsin

Grand Avenue Club, Inc.

Great Lakes Hemophilia Foundation

Horizon Home Care and Hospice

Milwaukee Area Health Education Center

Milwaukee Christian Center

National Alliance on Mental Illness (NAMI) Greater Milwaukee

National Multiple Sclerosis Society

Next Door Foundation

Pregnancy Help Center of Milwaukee, Inc.

St. Rose Youth and Family Center, Inc.

The Leukemia and Lymphoma Society

The TMJ Association

Transitional Living Services

Wheaton Franciscan Healthcare— St. Joseph Hospital

Wisconsin Breast Cancer Coalition

Word of Hope Ministries, Inc.

IMMIGRATION

Caritas for Children

Council for Spanish Speaking, Inc.

Council for the Spanish Speaking, Inc.

Lutheran Social Services

Milwaukee Christian Center

LITERACY

Artworks for Milwaukee

Audio and Braille Literacy Enhancement, Inc.

Bay View Community Center

Benedict Center, Inc.

Boys and Girls Clubs of Greater Milwaukee

Carmen High School of Science and Technology

COA Youth and Family Centers

Ebenezer Child Care from the Heart

Girl Scouts

Gray's Child Development Center

Hickman Preparatory School

Historic Milwaukee, Inc.

Hope House

Housing Authority of the City of Milwaukee

La Causa Family Resource Center

Milwaukee Achiever Literacy Services

Milwaukee Center for Independence

Milwaukee Christian Center

Milwaukee College Prep School

Milwaukee Public Library

Milwaukee Public Museum

North Point Lighthouse Friends, Inc.

Rethinking Schools

RSVP Senior Corps

Sponsor-a-Scholar

St. Charles Youth and Family Services, Inc.

St. Francis Children's Center

United Community Center/Centro de la Comunidad Unida

Walker's Point Center for the Arts

YMCA of Metropolitan Milwaukee

This list, as long as it is, doesn't even include opportunities to tackle issues such as political reform, homelessness, children and families, disaster relief, senior citizens, education, race relations, community building, consumer protection, economic development, or job training, all of which are categories nonprofits serve in most communities.

How can you pull up a list like this for your own town? There are a few ways:

Go to www.idealist.org.
Select Volunteer Opportunities.
Select an Area of Focus, your hometown, and any pertinent keywords.

You can also consult your town's volunteer center website (in Milwaukee, it's www.volunteermilwaukee.org). Some of them list their available volunteer opportunities. You can refine your search by choosing the duration of your project, your age group, and your interests.

Last but not least, go to VolunteerMatch at www.volunteermatch.org and conduct an advanced search.

Perhaps you noticed that some organizations pop up under several different headings. It's common for an organization's services or agenda to indirectly straddle more than one issue. Thus, a group that advocates for immigration reform might also have opportunities for someone who wants to teach English as a second language, or work with victims of domestic abuse, or provide family counseling, or offer nutritional and meal planning advice. We've said it before and we'll say it again, the opportunities for people to share what they know with others are endless.

KNOWING YOURSELF

To help you focus as you start to think about where you might find the greatest satisfaction, and where your time, money, or expertise might have the greatest effect, here are some other questions worth considering:

1. *What kind of gratification do you need to feel you've made an impact?* If you love children, what would give you the most satisfaction, direct service or indirect service? In other words, do you need to be in immediate contact with children—tutoring a student for three hours a week to ensure he or she moves up a grade—or would you be satisfied working behind the scenes—designing a newsletter that draws media attention to children's programs, staffing a phone bank to support a children's agency in getting more clients, making a donation so they can expand their programs' reach?

2. *What makes you feel connected to others or to a cause?* Do you need to be able to see the effects of your work in your community, or will you get an equal charge reading about your group's progress in the national newspaper? Will you gain the same satisfaction knowing that your contribution allows hundreds of schoolchildren in Ghana access to textbooks and a structurally sound building as you would if you could drive past the charter school you support and see the kids playing in their freshly paved and planted schoolyard?

TWO TYPES OF SERVICE

As you consider what issues you might like to get involved with, you should know that there are two ways in which idealists generally make their mark—through direct service or through indirect service (some positions are a blend of the two).

DIRECT SERVICE. Direct service generally occurs out in the "field." To participate in direct service is to have one-on-one contact with the beneficiaries of an organization's efforts. For many people, the opportunity to see for themselves how a nonprofit or even a socially responsible company makes a difference in the community or the lives of individuals is the main draw to civic engagement.

On the other hand, direct service can require a thick skin. It can mean coming face-to-face with other people's hardship, illness, or suffering. It's one thing to want to feed the poor; it's another thing to look into the eyes of a hungry child. We're not saying you shouldn't consider direct service if you can't stomach unpleasantness; clearly all direct service doesn't involve being a witness to suffering. But be careful to manage your expectations. People sometimes start their direct service with the idea that those they are serving are going to express gratitude for their efforts. You should expect volunteer managers and other people within the organization to be appreciative, but sometimes individuals within the community would rather not have to be in the position of being served, or may not be able or willing to articulate or display an appreciation for your work. Don't take on a position mentoring a sixteen-year-old if you dream of being that kid's hero. If that's the kind of emotional reward you're looking for (and a lot of us are), you'll probably be better off volunteering with small children, who are often more demonstrative, or at the local animal shelter.

It's also sometimes difficult to get closure with direct service, or to measure the impact of what you are doing. Direct service can be a one-shot task, like serving food on Wednesday nights at a soup kitchen, but often direct service projects are ongoing, which means it may not always be possible to look at what you have done and pinpoint an accomplished goal. You may even wonder if you've succeeded. If you're working with autistic children, it could be a long time before you see proof that your efforts are paying off in some way. If being able to quantify your service is important to you, you might be better off looking at indirect service opportunities.

That said, direct service can be a deeply rewarding experience. There's a reason why many people start volunteering for an organization and find themselves still volunteering there many years later—nonprofits are often joyful places to be.

INDIRECT SERVICE. Many people who work for nonprofits are involved in indirect service, the behind-the-scenes activities that keep an organization running. Accounting, Web design, building maintenance, staffing phone lines, ordering supplies—these tasks are the backbone of any nonprofit. For some volunteers, this kind of work isn't exciting or gratifying enough. But many people gain great satisfaction knowing that they play an important part in helping a nonprofit fulfill its mission. And an additional benefit is that they can point to a pile of letters ready to be mailed out, or a beautifully designed newsletter, or a freshly painted office, and say, "I did that."

3. *What issue is most on your mind right now?* Why? Is there something going on in your life that compels you to think about it?

- Is this a new issue to you, or have you long been following it? Say you are interested in childhood literacy. Did you just read something about the rates of illiteracy at the primary school level in the news? Are you watching a friend's child struggle with learning to read? Did you need special tutoring services to help you learn to read as a child?

- Are your feelings toward this issue vague or strong and well-defined? When you think about getting involved, does one issue immediately come to mind, like improving safety standards for car seats, or is it a more general sentiment, like wanting to make the world a better place for children?

4. *Are you more interested in giving money or giving time? How much and in what capacity?*

IT'S ALL GOOD

When you're thinking through these questions, resist the urge to compare yourself to other people. You might look at your neighbor and note that he has organized an all-volunteer landscaping committee for the struggling local elementary school, and he offers computer literacy tutorials for the third graders every Wednesday afternoon. Yet all you know for sure is that you'd like to help kids, and that you're not willing to give up your daily workout at the gym in order to do it. But the difference between what your neighbor gives and what you are ready to give isn't important. What is important is that you are ready to give. Whatever contributions materialize from that impulse will be of great value to you and to the group that you choose to work with.

You don't have to be a saint to make a difference. Sure—you can commit your professional life to a nonprofit. Or you can volunteer. You can serve on a board. You can make a donation. You can start your own socially responsible company. These are all excellent and equally valuable ways to contribute time, money, or expertise to the goal of making this world a better place. Regardless of which path you choose to take (and it's likely that over time you might take different ones) every one of them has the power not only to positively impact a cause you believe in, but to change your life for good.

IDEALISM IN ACTION

ONE OF MY LIFETIME GOALS IS TO BE AS GENEROUS AS I CAN BE. I AM NOT THE MOST BRILLIANT THINKER IN THE WORLD, SO I AM NOT GOING TO PUSH FORWARD THE FRONTIERS OF HUMAN KNOWLEDGE. NOR AM I ESPECIALLY AMBITIOUS IN MY CAREER, SO I AM NOT GOING TO BE THE CEO OF THE NEXT GOOGLE. HOWEVER, I DO HAVE MORAL AMBITION. I WOULD LIKE TO STRETCH MYSELF TO BE THE MOST GENEROUS PERSON I CAN BE. I THINK THAT IS IN MY POWER. EVEN IF I FAIL, IT CAN'T HURT TO TRY.

—Cliff Landesman, donor, volunteer, Trickle Up, Oxfam America, Natural Resources Defense Council, Lake Champlain Committee, Alaska Center for the Environment, WNYC, Pedals for Progress, among others; Brooklyn, New York

2

Nonprofit Basics

"The only ones among you who will be really happy are those who will have sought and found how to serve."

—ALBERT SCHWEITZER

Let's backtrack for a minute. You picked up this book because you're interested in making a difference in the world, and the first thing we do is point you in the direction of nonprofits. Why? What's so special about nonprofits?

A book that outlines the best ways to turn your good intentions into action would be incomplete without a chapter introducing the basics about nonprofits and other agencies that work for social benefit. So here it is, the one-stop, quick-read rundown of how nonprofits function. Familiarizing yourself with nonprofit terminology will make it easier for you to figure out where you'll maximize your impact and gain the most satisfaction from your experience. While there will never be just one way to do the work you want to do, these pages will help you to understand some of the more common similarities and differences among nonprofit organizations.

WHAT IS A NONPROFIT, ANYWAY?

AARP. The United States Olympic Committee. PBS. The Smithsonian Institution. American Automobile Association (AAA). Veterans of Foreign Wars (VFW). The Rock and Roll Hall of Fame. The Louisiana Disaster Recovery Foundation. The United Negro College Fund. The California Hospital Medical Center. The Museum of Modern Art. The University of Chicago. St. Austin Catholic Parish. You might recognize some of these names, and others are likely unfamiliar. Some are internationally known, others are local. They have little in common but for one thing: they are all nonprofits, and they represent the astounding diversity of options available to anyone who wants to contribute time, skill, or money toward a cause that matters to them.

What's in a Name?

People often dismiss nonprofits—they're a waste of time, they can't really make a difference, they are refuges for people who can't handle the "real world"—because of the common misperception that by definition they don't make any money. Well, that's certainly true about some of them, but that doesn't mean that nonprofits *can't* make money. Many do, in fact. But whether they make money or not, they can be as effective at achieving their goals as many for-profit companies. (We'll examine how later in this chapter and throughout the book.) Don't be fooled by the term "nonprofit"; it does not equal "insolvent," "ineffectual," or "inefficient."

Also, when reading about nonprofits, you'll often see references to them being part of something called the nonprofit "sector," as well as the independent sector, charitable sector, voluntary sector, and civil society. Nonprofits are also sometimes lumped into the "third sector" to differentiate them from organizations in the other two "sectors" of the economy, the private and the public. The private sector refers to businesses or for-profit entities, whether local like Bronx Carpet Cleaning, national like Bed Bath & Beyond, or international like IKEA. The public sector refers to those services administered or controlled by the government, such as the City of Albuquerque's Solid Waste Management Department, the New Mexico Public Regulation Commission, and the U.S. Social Security Administration.

We're not going to use any of these terms, because using them may imply that there is a competition running between these three different branches of society and government, and that's just not the case. No one is launching quarterly meetings saying, "OK, team, how are we going to stick it to those nonprofits?" For-profits are not evil and nonprofits aren't inherently better than government agencies. Each has its own purpose and best practice.

In addition, many people in the nonprofit world actually

chafe at the use of the word "nonprofit" because it's a term that places undue emphasis on an organization's tax-exempt status (which we'll explain in a minute), not the good the group does through its mission. The important thing about the West Seattle Food Bank is not that it's tax exempt, nor does tax status matter when it comes to organizations who stop people from driving drunk, or prevent genocide, or read to the blind. As nonprofits continue to evolve, it's probable that we will see more animated debates over the right language to use to describe this complex and ever-shifting arena.

A nonprofit organization—also called not-for-profit, or abbreviated as NPO—is defined most simply as a private group formed to serve public purposes.

Opinions differ over the distinguishing characteristics of a nonprofit organization, but the most widely accepted authoritative list was drawn up by Lester Salamon, director of the John Hopkins Center for Civil Society Studies and a leading expert on nonprofits in the United States and around the world. He defines a nonprofit as:

1. An organization
2. Private, as opposed to governmental
3. Non-profit-distributing
4. Self-governing
5. Voluntary
6. Of public benefit[3]

501(C)(3) ORGANIZATIONS

There are so many nonprofits—approximately 1.48 million in this country alone[4]—that choosing the one you want to get involved with can seem daunting. Actually, though, you've probably already participated in an activity sponsored by a nonprofit, maybe even without realizing it. If you ever played Little League or joined the Girl Scouts, staffed a booth at a community fair or festival, or attended a play in an alternative theater space, it's likely that the team or fair or theatre troupe was a nonprofit organization. Furthermore, if you paid dues, bought a ticket, or were charged admission, you supported that organization. Many schools, credit unions, social service agencies, and economic-development groups are nonprofits, too. For more specific examples, see the Appendix at the end of the book.

Nonprofits differ in size, wealth, mission, values, and style of operation. There are several kinds of tax-exempt organizations defined in the federal tax code, but the one that is familiar to most people is charities, identified by the tax code 501(c)(3). It is to these that we'll give the most attention in this book.

> A comprehensive introduction to the way the IRS administers the tax code for exempt organizations is presented in Publication 557, found on the IRS website at www.irs.gov/pub/irs-pdf/p557.pdf.

Assuming they meet certain federal standards, they are not only exempt from paying federal income tax, but they are tax exempt under Section 501(c)(3) of the Tax Code, which is the IRS's cryptic shorthand for stipulating that they may receive tax-deductible gifts and contributions from individuals and are eligible for grants from many foundations. Remember our discussion in Chapter 1 about the financial benefits of philanthropy? This is one of them: usually people who donate money or valuable items to a group that has been identified as a 501(c)(3) are entitled to deduct the amount of that contribution from their taxable income. It's one very important feature that differentiates a 501(c)(3) from other tax-exempt organizations.

There are a few important rules about what a 501(c)(3) organization can and can't do:

1. It must dedicate all its assets and income to the mission, and cannot pay any profit to stockholders or owners.
2. Its mission must state what the tax code lists as "exempt purposes"—religious, charitable, scientific, educational, and literary activities, plus a few others. Once the mission is adopted, it can only be changed by following a careful process of amendment of the organization's charter.
3. It may lobby for causes or speak out on issues at the legislative level, but it must not impede or contribute to any electoral campaign.
4. It must report annually to the federal government (and maybe state or local as well) on its activities and finances. These reports must be made available to the public; they are often posted online.

5. It can earn a limited amount of business income from activities that are unrelated to its exempt purposes, but such income will be taxed at the federal level at the same rates that apply to for-profit corporations.

WHAT'S THE DIFFERENCE BETWEEN NONPROFITS AND FOR-PROFITS?

Sometimes people judge nonprofits more favorably than commercial businesses because of their do-good mission as well as other differences between them. We at Idealist.org don't think these differences make one kind of organization inherently better than the other; however, it's good to understand the differences, since they are often the reason why many individuals seek out nonprofits—and create them—in the first place. First, unlike a for-profit/commercial enterprise, a nonprofit's reason for being is not to make money for an owner, shareholder, or investor. In fact, no one can claim ownership of a nonprofit, so unlike a business, which will see its assets liquidated and distributed among owners or shareholders if it fails, a nonprofit that goes out of business can only redistribute its assets to another nonprofit.

A second key distinction between nonprofits and for-profits is, of course, tax status. A business or company is required to pay state and federal income taxes on any profit it makes. Not so for a 501(c)(3) nonprofit. It receives a tax-exempt status in acknowledgment of its existence for the greater good.

The lack of ownership and its 501(c)(3) status often serve to make people feel they can trust an organization's motives and management, which in turn reassures someone interested in donating time, money, or expertise that their contribution will be appropriately used for a good cause. Only by establishing this sense of trust will a nonprofit get the financial and physical (in the form of volunteers) support it needs to survive.

NONPROFITS OR FOR-PROFITS—IS THERE NO IN-BETWEEN?

As a matter of fact, there is. A new generation of entrepreneurs is beginning to question the strict division between the mission of for-profit companies and those of nonprofits. With pressure building on traditional for-profit entities to contribute more to the public welfare and the environment, and nonprofits battling for dwindling resources and donations, and under increasing financial scrutiny, entrepreneurs are seeing opportunities to launch "social enterprises," mission-based, profit-oriented businesses often called for-benefit companies, hybrids, or triple-bottom-line companies (because they measure their success in their positive impact on people, the planet, and profit). These operate as both nonprofit and for-profit. They are not exclusively constrained by obligations to shareholders yet are still able to adopt corporate methods unavailable to most nonprofits. Hybrid organizations can range from neighborhood restaurants that feature locally grown produce or raised meat, to big companies like Patagonia, which lists its mission statement as

"Build the best product, cause no unnecessary harm, use business to inspire and implement solutions to the environmental crisis." For many, hybrids could provide the solution to balancing one's need to do good in the world while still enjoying the financial rewards of capitalism.

> With the emergence of for-benefit companies and rising interest in corporate social responsibility (CSR), many companies are starting to fold words like "organic," "green," and "sustainable" into their marketing materials and product lines. In Chapter 9, we'll discuss the implications of this trend and offer suggestions for how you can ascertain which companies are serious about committing to more socially and environmentally responsible business practices, and which ones are supporting the idea with lip service and spin.

For now, though, tax laws still fall strictly along for-profit and nonprofit lines. The laws severely limit the ability of many hybrids to stay true to their principles and still increase profits, without eventually selling to a company that may not have the same set of values at the center of their work. (Ben & Jerry's, for example, sold to Unilever in 2000.) At the rate this movement is growing, however, those laws may be in for an overhaul.

WHERE DOES THE MONEY COME FROM?

So if a nonprofit isn't in the business of making money for owners or shareholders, doesn't generally abide by capitalist philosophy, and hasn't found that proverbial moneymaking tree, where does its cash flow come from? As we've already mentioned, nonprofits rely upon financial donations from private citizens, corporations, and government agencies. These contributions can take many forms, and it would behoove anyone who gets involved with a nonprofit to be familiar with these terms, since it's likely you will often hear them discussed:

Grant is the general term used to describe gifts of money given to tax-exempt nonprofit organizations. Anyone— individuals, corporations, foundations, government agencies— can bestow a grant upon a nonprofit. The government is by far the largest grant maker, though it usually disburses the money through state and local agencies and leaves it up to them to decide who gets what.

Another source of income for a nonprofit might be an **endowment**. In this case, a donor provides funds to a nonprofit for investment purposes only. The nonprofit is expected to keep the principal intact and either spend the interest on its programs or reinvest its earnings. Endowments are major sources of income for universities, for example.

It might be easy to stereotype some nonprofits as anti–big business, but most will acknowledge that companies represent an important resource. **Corporate contributions** make up a significant portion of the total amount of money donated to nonprofits every year. Many companies have established corporate gift programs to support organizations working on issues of particular concern to them, such as Barnes & Noble, whose corporate contribution program supports agencies that focus on literacy, education, or the arts, and Genentech, which makes donations to groups working in health care and science. Others simply decide to support one or two issues where they believe they can make a difference. So JCPenney offers grants to organizations working toward improving and developing curriculum-based after-school care, and Kodak supports programs dedicated to community revitalization efforts. Many companies will also give significant dollars to a variety of organizations in a certain geographic location, typically where they are headquartered or where they have a large number of employees.

Foundations are second only to the government in the amount of money they distribute to nonprofits. Foundations are formed to distribute grants to agencies and individuals working toward scientific, educational, cultural, religious, or other charitable purposes.

A CHALLENGING LANDSCAPE IN YOUR FAVOR

The challenges of operating a nonprofit have become significantly more difficult due to increased regulatory scrutiny and a more crowded environment of organizations with overlapping missions. It used to be that a bunch of friends could band together on a whim and call themselves a nonprofit. Regulations weren't as strict, and the public's expectations weren't as stiff. All that has changed now, in large part because of the Internet. Individuals and groups interested in a nonprofit expect immediate access to information and clear examples of what the organization has accomplished and its plans for the future (although it's not always easy to deliver that transparency, especially for small or older organizations).

> One of the reasons Idealist.org exists (as well as other online resource centers) is to address this problem of transparency. By serving as an intermediary between individuals and organizations, we allow the free-flowing exchange of information that is so crucial to enabling idealists to fulfill their desire to contribute something to their community, and to organizations posting the information that will attract the right idealists to their doors.

Money, too, is of course an issue. Every nonprofit is forced to creatively problem-solve to address the shortfalls inevitably caused during times of shifting government priorities or a weakened economy. And while they'd all say that more money would help, ultimately more money only offers a temporary fix. Organizations may need more fish in the short run, but in the long run they could really use someone with better fishing technique. That's where you come in.

The struggle for nonprofits to address these increasing pressures presents great opportunities for you. Nonprofits are as eager to draw in talented, energetic people to work with them as any other organization. Revealing the myriad ways in which you can maximize your impact on a nonprofit's mission through your time, skills, or donations, while fulfilling your own needs, will be the focus for the rest of this section of the book.

IDEALISM IN ACTION

ONE OF THE THINGS I THINK IS CRUCIAL FOR ORGANIZATIONS TO REMEMBER IS THE VERY IMPORTANT ROLE THAT NONPROFITS PLAY IN ENABLING PEOPLE TO BE ABLE TO EXPRESS THEIR VALUES. GIVING PEOPLE A WAY TO CONNECT TO A NONPROFIT IN A REAL WAY, AND MAKE TANGIBLE THEIR COMMITMENT TO DOING GOOD, IS A SUBTLE AND COMPLICATED COMMUNICATION TASK. ORGANIZATIONS THAT DO IT WELL ARE LIKELY TO PROSPER BECAUSE THEY'RE LIKELY TO GET PEOPLE TO STICK WITH THEM. THEY SUCCEED BECAUSE THEY CONVEY TO PEOPLE HOW THEIR ORGANIZATION AFFECTS AND IMPROVES THE WORLD. I GUESS THEY ARE DOING BETTER MARKETING, FOR LACK OF A BETTER WORD THAT GETS THE POINT ACROSS. THAT'S NOT TO SAY THAT PASSION DOESN'T COUNT, BUT THE MOST EFFECTIVE WAY A NONPROFIT CAN PROVE THEIR VISION COMMITMENT IS GOING TO BE BY TAKING A MORE BUSINESS-LIKE APPROACH.

—Putnam Barber, senior researcher, Idealist.org; Seattle, Washington

3

Where Do I Fit In?

The diversity of options available within the world of non-profits can be staggering to anyone trying to decide where to contribute his or her time, money, or expertise. Staggering in a good way, because you have so many opportunities to figure out what's going to make you happy. One thing to keep in mind is that there's no rule saying you have to pick only one path. There are ways to combine your multiple interests and skills; for example, an advantage to donating money is that even a person of modest means can support several different causes by writing checks; if you want to better understand the big picture, joining a board can give you excellent information and insight; if you don't want to narrow down your interests, a series of onetime volunteer opportunities can allow you to help many organizations and never be bored. Regardless of whether you want to explore several organizations or concentrate on only one, the following information can help you get a stronger sense of what you want to do.

There are several things you need to consider about a nonprofit before deciding if it is the best fit for you. Ultimately, you're going to choose a nonprofit based on a particular combination of your interests, resources, and needs. And you don't want to find yourself facing a blank wall once your current needs are filled. You want to see open doors, and lots of them. Knowing what differentiates nonprofits will help you figure out what is a good fit for you right now; knowing these differences will also help you figure out what will be a good fit for you later when your interests, resources, and needs change.

THINGS TO CONSIDER

The Nonprofit's Cause

If you answered the questions we posed at the end of Chapter 1, by now you should have an idea of which subjects matter most to you. Thus, if you're passionate about good eating and nutrition, you might narrow your search to agencies that work with families to promote healthy eating habits, or programs that want to improve the quality of school cafeterias, or a food bank. You might be a pharmaceutical rep, but if you write poetry on the side you might look for agencies that promote literacy or teach creative writing. You can also choose an agency that offers this service to the general public, or works with a specific group, such as inmates or recent immigrants. Maybe you've discovered that you want to more fully incorporate your faith into your life, so you might investigate programs sponsored by a synagogue, mosque, church, or other place of worship.

Local or Global?

Another thing to think about is the scope of your ambitions. Some people are anxious to improve the conditions of their immediate community and wish to have individual relationships with the beneficiaries of their efforts. Others are drawn to the clout of a nationally or internationally recognized organization or are eager to eradicate problems at the global level. Do you want to donate to or volunteer or work for a nonprofit with a local, statewide/regional, national, or international mission?

Whatever issue is on your mind or whatever interest you'd like to pursue, there's probably already a nonprofit that exists for it both locally and globally. Think about the organizations and institutions you're already familiar with, that you admire, or that tackle issues that matter to you. Many are probably nonprofits. Below is a sample of the kinds of organizations you might find where you live:

Local Nonprofits. Houston Food Bank, Portland Children's Museum, Bosnian-Herzegovinian Community Club of Boise, Metro Atlanta Task Force for the Homeless, Ojai Valley Youth Foundation

State Nonprofits. Clean Water Action of Rhode Island, Alaska Radio Mission, ACLU of New Mexico, American Red Cross of Greater Idaho, Oklahoma Goodwill Industries, Middle Tennessee Mental Health Institute

Regional/National Nonprofits. Girl Scouts of America, United States Holocaust Memorial Museum, American Heart Association, National Football League, Better Business Bureau, Southwest Housing Solutions, Pacific Northwest Ballet

International Nonprofits. Feed the Children, World Vision International, Ford Foundation, Amnesty International, Rotary, Catholic Relief Services, International Association for Religious Freedom

It's easy to assume that getting involved with small, local, grassroots organizations is the best way to have a lot of direct contact with individuals or with your community. But in fact the opposite can be true. Large organizations with staff and infrastructure may have more opportunities available for you to go out into the field or to tailor your volunteer work to your interests. A small group may have already assigned work involving direct contact to a few individuals, so what they really need is people to help them with the day-to-day work that keeps such organizations going, such as welcoming visitors, stocking shelves, and handling correspondence. Every organization's needs differ, of course, so the best course of action is never to discount any nonprofit simply because it's large and national or small and grassroots.

Organizational Culture

When deciding where to contribute your service, don't forget to ask yourself the really important questions "Do I like this place?" "Is this a group where I fit in?" A good indication will be how you feel about the nonprofit's organizational culture.

Are you more comfortable in a formal or informal environment? Are you looking to join an established organization or a start-up? Do you mind being a small fish in a very big pond, or do you prefer to have more visibility and influence on the organization as a whole? The formality of an organization's structure, its age, its size, and even how it uses technology matter because if you're planning to get involved with a nonprofit, you want to spend your time with people whose company you enjoy. And if you're researching the right place to make a donation, you want to feel that your money is being well spent by people whose decisions you respect. An agency that has been in existence for fifty years or more is going to have a significantly different kind of culture than one that got started two years ago. And an organization with a formal structure is not going to have the same feel as one with a more informal approach to management and problem-solving. The controlled chaos and inherent uncertainty that come with never knowing how much money will be in the bank from month to month can be exciting to some people, terrifying to others. You may decide that you're only comfortable working with a proven, well-established organization, one with a recognizable name and maybe even a marketing budget. Or you may be searching to inject your life with a little bit of unpredictability, or exhilarated by the idea of joining forces with a new, untested group where all the rules have yet to be written.

Four Cultural Categories

We've identified four categories into which many, though by no means all, organizations often fall. They should provide a useful framework as you analyze the structure of any group that piques your interest.

Working with a **formal** organization may feel similar to working in a traditional office environment. It's possible its hierarchy and daily schedule will have a more corporate feel than you might anticipate from a nonprofit. For example, an organization with a staff of twenty is located in the state capital. Staff members frequently meet with their local state representatives and speak on the news about energy issues. They pay a lot of attention to keeping the local media involved in their activities and getting out weekly press releases. Volunteers for the organization have very limited interaction with the executive director, who is often away at meetings. Volunteers may be pressed to call constituents, or if they're lucky, be asked to go to the Hill, so they are expected to leave their flip-flops at home and present themselves with an appropriately sober and buttoned-down look.

Though some people look to the nonprofit world as an escape from such formal corporate culture, others find comfort in its familiarity. For some, the structure and rules of a formal nonprofit indicate reliability and stability, a place where real, measurable work gets done and where they feel confident their efforts will pay off.

An **informal** organization may better reflect the environment a lot of people expect from a nonprofit. For example, an organization with a staff of twenty is located in the state's largest city. The dress code is relaxed—you'll rarely see anyone wearing a tie—but when financial donors or the press visit, people slip on khakis. Job titles and roles are not cut-and-dried; staff and volunteers may be expected to take on responsibilities that aren't necessarily in their job descriptions, embracing an ethos of "If you see it needs doing, do it," which explains why you'll see everyone from new hires up to the executive director lifting boxes and making copies. The physical layout of the office is open and therefore noisy and cluttered, but also conducive to collaboration and interaction. Staff members often meet with clients at their office, in the field, or at impromptu events at the local community center.

While some people may be intimidated by the apparent lack of focus or haphazard assignment of tasks at an informal organization, others might find the communal attitude makes them feel that their contribution, no matter what it is, is valuable.

The internal culture of an organization may also reflect their external approach to the community. Pay attention to the way the group promotes itself through advertising or marketing materials. This will give you a clue as to how you, as a representative of the nonprofit, will be expected to present yourself to the community. Are you comfortable interacting with people in this way?

While it's not always the case that **established** agencies are also more formal ones, age and structure do often go together. An established organization might look like this: A staff of fifty working for an organization that has been serving the residents of the state's second-largest city since 1915. The annual Halloween party is one of the highest-profile events of the year, and board members include the university president, partners from the biggest local law and accounting firms, and a local TV broadcaster. The group's summer-school and after-school tutoring programs are mainstays of the community. They have had years to develop relationships with the directors of the local colleges and religious congregations, which ensures a steady supply of interns and volunteers.

The good thing about older organizations is that they have had time to figure out what works for them and what doesn't. They've had interns and volunteers for years, so they likely have an orientation process in place. They have a track record. It's also likely that because of this track record there may be little opportunity for creativity, and the group may be resistant to change and not particularly open to a newcomer's input. Like anyone, the older a group gets, the more it can become set in its ways. This will especially be the case if the group has well-established sources of funding, and perhaps annual events that guarantee a certain cash flow.

Emerging organizations will likely still be struggling to bring in those much-needed dollars; they are still building the relationships that are crucial to providing the revenue stream necessary to any nonprofit's survival. But such struggles are often accompanied by a sense of energy and a can-do spirit that may be harder to find at older institutions. An emerging organization might look like this: A staff of five working for the past three years in a community that houses one of the outposts of the state university. An environmental organization founded by two friends who graduated from the university, and so the nonprofit has been able to get the school to provide some financial support. The staff relies on their campus connections, knowledge of social media, and other recent graduates for both funds and volunteers.

An emerging group will probably be much smaller than one that has had years to build its reputation and advertising budget, and therefore the people involved might be forced to wear many different hats. This means there may be a lot of opportunity for your creative input and chances for you to influence the nonprofit's future. For example, if you are one of their first volunteers, they may allow you to experiment with various approaches to your projects or even to the community so they can see what works and what doesn't. For people using their volunteer experience as resume fodder or for networking reasons, contributing time or expertise to a young nonprofit could represent an excellent opportunity to impress. And young nonprofits often experience growth spurts, which mean that the chances are good that a volunteer could be presented with a job offer.

Four Influential Factors

Regardless of what category a nonprofit falls into, you'll want to be aware of several important factors that will strongly influence your experience with an organization.

Size can make a difference, of course. A large institution may feel impersonal or impressive. A small one may feel claustrophobic or cozy. Then there are organizations that are less defined by their size than by who works for them. An all-volunteer group, such as Heart of Sailing, which teaches sailing to children with developmental disabilities, is going to have a much different organizational culture than an agency with a paid staff.

Technology, too, affects the organizational culture of nonprofits. There are many organizations that have embraced the digital age and incorporated everything the Web has to offer—email, podcasts, social sites, chat rooms, blogs—into an interactive environment that allows volunteers, paid staff, and the community at large to communicate, comment, and exchange information at will. There are probably an equal number of agencies that only see a website as a place to post their brochures online. Both approaches get the job done, but a true technophile might be frustrated by a perceived Ludditism on the part of the latter group. (On the other hand, perhaps the lack of such technology provides the perfect opportunity for the techie to show the organization how to take advantage of what the Web has to offer!)

> **Our day-to-day culture emphasizes mutual respect, constant learning and innovation, nimbleness, high-quality standards for our work, and a bit of irreverence. I love it! I believe that a good fit with an organization's culture is one of the biggest determinants of satisfaction, and I feel very lucky to be in this environment.**
>
> —Chris Tebben, executive director,
> Grantmakers for Education; Portland, Oregon

That said, there are no absolutes. Just because an organization is older or larger or more established doesn't mean that it necessarily will be any less innovative, entrepreneurial, or effective than an emerging nonprofit. In fact, be sure not to take some of the old stalwarts for granted. They've been around a long time for a reason.

Then there are **trends**. Causes can often become trendy. In the 1960s it was Vietnam. In the 1980s it was AIDS. In this first decade of the millennium it would seem that environmentalism is the hot topic of the day. The catastrophic events in Darfur, too, have received an enormous amount of attention in the past few years. People are naturally going to be attracted to the issues that receive a lot of buzz and that the press makes easily accessible through sound bites and celebrity testimonials. We're not saying that because a cause is popular you should look elsewhere when considering where to spend your time or money. If you're looking for a short-term opportunity, this will probably work out well for you. But if you're looking to get involved in something long-term, we'd like to caution you to be careful before climbing aboard the popular bandwagon. Maybe a lot of people you know are involved in a particular organization and want you to join them, and that could be exciting and fun and a great opportunity for sharing a worthwhile experience with people you like. But think deeply before committing to a cause that's popular but doesn't necessarily resonate with you. You'll get a lot more out of your experience if you contribute to an organization that means something to you personally, whether it's a new problem or one that people have been battling for a hundred years.

In addition, nonprofits themselves can sometimes get overwhelmed by their own popularity. Some are so accustomed to accepting offers of support from anyone who expresses an urge to contribute service that even when they experience a surge of interest they don't realize they lack the capacity to use everyone who wants to volunteer with them. They respond to your inquiry by telling you to come in, but they may not actually be in a position to use you in a way that's productive. For example, many of the organizations that are serving New Orleans post-Katrina are having a hard time utilizing all the people who want to contribute. If you're interested in working for a popular nonprofit or one that has recently received a lot of attention, be sure to ask specific questions about how they plan to make your experience there worthwhile.

Last, don't underestimate the important effect a nonprofit's

reputation will have on you, even after your time of service. It's easy to assume that people will be impressed that you have donated your time or expertise to a cause, any cause; after all, altruism is admirable, right? Yet it's important to recognize that by aligning yourself with a nonprofit you are also aligning yourself with that nonprofit's brand. If you are including your service to a nonprofit on your resume, whether as a volunteer or board member, be aware that it will affect how people perceive you even before they meet you. Let's say you love animals and take the opportunity to volunteer with PETA even though you're ambivalent about some of their tactics. For you, the volunteer opportunity is just a chance to get some experience under your belt before deciding whether you want to work full-time for an animal rights nonprofit. But later, upon learning about your service to PETA, some of the more established, less radically inclined animal rights organizations may perceive you as a poor fit for them even though you're not. That's not to say that there's anything wrong with volunteering for (or donating to) PETA. The point is that where you get your volunteer, board, or work experience matters, and you must recognize that not every service opportunity will be right for your goals. Be prepared to share with future interviewers what you got from the experience that can be of benefit to them. For example, PETA is an exceptional marketer, so the next time you meet with a volunteer manager you might discuss how the marketing experience you gained with PETA may be beneficial to her organization.

Does organizational culture really matter this much? Not for everyone. For some, the culture of an organization won't make a bit of difference to their contribution. Yet other people are extremely sensitive to their environment, and it will impact how comfortable they feel within the organization and whether they can identify with it. You could consider your investigation into a nonprofit the same way you might consider a planning a trip to Tahiti. You might stay in a posh hotel, you might prefer a hostel, or maybe you will be satisfied with a sleeping bag on the beach. Regardless, as long as you're comfortable, it's going to be a fabulous trip.

GETTING IN THE KNOW

It might seem like a tall order to weigh this long list of things to consider—cause and scope and the various categories and factors that make up organizational culture—but it's worth it. You might be wondering, though, just how you are supposed to find out this information? The best way is the old-fashioned route—a visit. The first time you set foot in the organization's office shouldn't be the day you show up for volunteer training. Stop by the office at a time when no one is prepared to show off the nonprofit's best side. You could also ask for an informational interview with someone already doing the work you're interested in. But even if you can't make it to the office or headquarters, you can attend training seminars or events sponsored by the organization. You can go to their website. You can ask them to send you reading materials in the mail. And whenever possible, try to talk to former volunteers and employees. Every organization has a public face and a private one, and no one will be better able to reveal whether those two faces are in synch with your needs than someone who has already been on the inside.

AT A GLANCE

If you're interested in donating time or expertise, or if you're thinking of a career in the nonprofit world, it might be helpful to create a chart as you start researching the various organizations you think might provide good opportunities for you. This will help you easily spot which ones are the most likely to suit all of your needs.

ORGANIZA-TION	ISSUE	GEO-GRAPHIC RANGE (Local, state, nat'l., int'l.)	DIRECT CONTACT OPPORTUNITIES (Yes/No)	TIME COMMITMENT (Once a week, once a month, etc.)	ORGANIZATIONAL CULTURE (Formal, large/informal, small/formal, small/informal, small/emerging, established, etc.)
Girl Scouts of America	Children and Youth; Community Building	National, with local chapters	Yes	Varied	Formal, large, established
Heart of Sailing	Education; Mental Health; Sports and Recreation	U.S., France, Canada; regional programs in U.S.	Yes	Mostly weekends	Emerging, still growing
Grand Canyon Association	Education; Research and Science; Environment and Ecology	Local	Mostly paid positions	Full and part-time; Contract	Established, small, formal

What's the point of donating any resource—time, money, or expertise—if you don't gain a sense of pride and satisfaction afterward? Sure, the organization will benefit—for a little while. But then what happens when you get bored, or you get tired of the last-minute deadlines being thrown at you, or you admit that the organization has an agenda that you're trying to ignore?

You want your contribution to be sustainable, something you look forward to and enjoy talking about. After all, the more you love the way your contribution makes you feel, the more you'll want to share your experience with others, and then who knows? Maybe you'll inspire someone else to give a little bit, too.

IDEALISM IN ACTION

MY FIRST CAREER WAS IN A LAW FIRM AND IN CORPORATE LEGAL DEPARTMENTS, THEN I MOVED FROM BEING A LAWYER TO THE BUSINESS SIDE. I'M THE CLASSIC LIBERAL ARTS MAJOR, JACK OF ALL TRADES.

I KNEW TTN WAS ENTREPRENEURIAL AND COMFORTABLE WITH SOMEONE FROM A CORPORATE BACKGROUND. I LIKE THE CULTURE A LOT—TTN IS GOOD AT LEARNING AND EVOLVING QUICKLY. THE SENSE OF MISSION AND OPPORTUNITIES

TO HAVE SOCIAL IMPACT ARE GREAT. FOR ME, WORKING AT A MICRO-NONPROFIT (BUDGET UNDER $500,000) IS GREAT BECAUSE THERE'S LIMITED BUREAUCRACY. I'M ABLE TO HAVE A BIG INFLUENCE.

—Betsy Werley, executive director, The Transition Network; New York, New York

4

All Experience Is Relevant

How often have you sat down and made a list of all the things you're good at? We're not just talking about the job experiences you'd list on a resume (although those should be included); we're talking about *all* the things you're good at, like storytelling, or ice hockey, or gardening, or listening, or soothing babies, or planning parties, or math. Believe it or not, your skills, talents, and gifts—those you were born with and those you have developed—can often be channeled into a rewarding project with a nonprofit. Since most people tend to overlook the richness and diversity of their life experience, this chapter will guide you through a self-assessment process to make sure you look at yourself from every flattering angle. You'll also find examples for loads of ways nonprofits can take advantage of even the most seemingly mundane talents.

For those of you interested in applying for a job with a nonprofit, in Chapter 11 we'll explore how to incorporate your self-assessment into your job hunt, but even if you're thinking of volunteering, serving on a board, or making a monetary donation, consider this chapter a unique opportunity to take full inventory of everything you have to offer, not just to a non-profit, but to the world.

JOB SKILLS

Your job, of course, is a key place to look when putting together a list of your skills. There are two kinds of skills: formal job skills—the ones you have trained for, often even before you begin your job—and informal job skills—the ones you have developed in response to your job requirements and working conditions. Let's say you're an advertising copywriter. First, think about the skills you have trained for in order to perform your job well. You probably took some writing classes in college, and you probably learned to build a portfolio through your school's Communications or Media Department. Maybe you interned with a local ad agency to build your resume before heading out into the job market. But once you got your first job, you probably realized that there was a lot more to being a copywriter than just good writing skills. To stay competitive and up-to-date in your field, you have probably learned about graphic design; print, TV, online, and radio production; and computer programs such as Word, Flash, Adobe Photoshop, and Illustrator. In addition, though, you have also developed your informal job skills—how to negotiate, how to delegate, how to finesse client relations, how to make concise yet inspiring presentations. You have also had to stay aware of pop culture trends and keep an eye on youth-oriented markets, such as social networking sites like MySpace and Facebook.

Or maybe you're a financial planner. You probably studied algebra, statistics, and forecasting. You have probably gone to business school, either direct from your undergraduate studies, or perhaps by way of a stint with a law firm. In B-school you would have learned how to research and write briefs and argue logically. But there are informal skills that a good financial planner must understand that can be addressed in school but can only be mastered on the job: organizational behavior, how to lead a team to a decision, how to assess and handle different personalities. You find that you can explain an investment strategy to a client in clear, simple terms and the client can still look at you blankly. This doesn't mean you're wrong and it doesn't mean the client is dumb—it means you have to figure out how to speak his language. All of this knowledge, whether formal or informal, is exceedingly valuable and can be put to use by a nonprofit.

> **Everything you know can be taught to someone else. You've worked in an office, an experience which you and most of the people you know take for granted. But to some people, that experience is valuable. You could teach them workplace skills, appropriate dress, proper office and phone etiquette, or how to work a computer. Don't discount anything you do as mundane or old hat—to someone else, it's gold.**
>
> —Greg Nelson, volunteer, Native American Youth and Family Center (NAYA) and Oregon Native American Business and Entrepreneurial Network (ONABEN); Lake Oswego, Oregon

Some of you might wince when you see that we're asking you to list job skills and training. Students, parents who have taken time off to raise children or who never joined the workforce, and maybe even some people who have been in the same job for a long time, or who hold down jobs but don't consider themselves on a career track, might automatically think that they don't have any relevant skills to offer a nonprofit. Think again.

Students. Remember that any work experience, any experience at all, counts. That job waiting tables at Bennigan's, the babysitting gigs, manning the front desk at Ryder truck rental, digging ditches on your uncle's construction site—in every one of those jobs, you learned to do something you didn't know how to do before. Maybe it was how to calculate numbers quickly in your head, or maybe bartending skills. Write it down. Maybe it was CPR. Maybe it was how to manage a national tracking system, or deal with customer service issues and credit fraud. Write it down.

How about on-campus jobs? Have you supervised the computer lab? Given school tours to incoming freshmen? Worked as an RA? Served meals in one of the dorm kitchens? Taken leadership roles in school groups?

Stay-at-Home Parents. It's rare to encounter anyone who doesn't acknowledge the tremendous amount of work it takes to be a stay-at-home parent. Ironically, often the people who overlook how much they accomplish in a given day or week are the stay-at-home parents themselves. Much to the dismay of many first-time mothers and fathers, you don't get a how-to manual the day you begin raising a child, and there are few formal skills that you can train for to do this particular job well. But your informal job skill list is surely impressive. Over the years you've probably played some or all of the following roles, often simultaneously: negotiator, guidance counselor, cook, coach, tutor, event planner, fund-raiser, and project coordinator. There are certainly many others you can come up with on your own.

Next, think about the activities you have been involved with through your children's school or clubs. Did you start or do you participate in the local chapter of a mother's group? Are you involved in the PTA? Did you lead the fund-raising effort for the new playground equipment at your child's school? Have you taken a leadership role in your son's Boy Scout troop or your daughter's volleyball team? Are you on a committee to improve the academic performance of your local school? Write it down.

Whatever you do, don't forget to write down those "soft skills" at which many parents excel (though not necessarily every day or at the same time), for example, time management, organization, attention to detail, patience, multitasking, and focusing in the midst of chaos.

Let us remind you, too, that even if you have been out of the workforce for a while, those professional skills you gained while employed are still valuable to a nonprofit. You may need to update certain credentials or certifications, take another class or two, but you certainly won't be starting over again from scratch.

HOBBIES

What do you do for fun? Yes, the skills you have developed while learning a hobby or favorite pastime should be included in your skills evaluation. As we've already noted, photographers, visual artists, and writers can find excellent opportunities to contribute time and expertise to a nonprofit. But imagine, also, how eager a local after-school program would be to take advantage of your soccer skills, or what a great contribution you could make to Doggone Safe (which teaches about dog bite prevention) or Canine Companions for Independence if you have raised and trained hunting dogs since childhood. Someone with theater training who is comfortable performing and reading aloud or an avid bookworm might find a terrific opportunity with Recording for the Blind and Dyslexic. If you don't go anywhere without your iPod, you might be a perfect person to help out at Words, Beats, and Life. If you live for the days when weather permits you to take your boat out, Heart of Sailing or Sea Scouts might be a great fit for you.

ACCESS

What do you have access to? Do you have a boat? Take residents of the local senior citizen's center on a cruise. A car? Deliver food for Meals on Wheels. Did you build your own darkroom? Offer to teach a class to a teen runaway shelter. Whom do you have access to? Maybe you have a friend with a theater company who could loan out their stage. Your roommate does PR for the Knicks. Your father owns horses. These are all valuable resources, whether you're doing board service or skilled or unskilled volunteering.

NATURAL TALENTS

What are you naturally good at? The skills we're asking you to think of here aren't even necessarily skills at all. You might consider them more character traits. Regardless, everyone has certain talents that spring from just being who they are. Are you fiercely organized, the kind of person whose idea of heaven is a free weekend to organize your closets and haul out loads of clutter? Have you thought about helping sort through donations to your local Goodwill? Are you particularly empathic, the friend everyone turns to when they need an objective, attentive listener? You might offer your time at a switchboard for runaways. Are you bilingual? You can help local immigrant groups with language training classes. Do you have a special bond with most animals or children? Are you an excellent speller, a math whiz, a problem-solver? Do you love to make lists and itineraries? Are you a natural entertainer, the life of every party? Do you have perfect pitch? Do not limit yourself as you think about what you have to give—that is the key to creating a fulfilling, even exciting experience.

LIFE EXPERIENCE

Life experience, while not technically a skill, gift, or talent, has a profound influence on what draws individuals to one non-profit or another. Think about the environment you grew up in. Did it provide experiences that might help you relate to people in a certain community? Are you a survivor of an illness or accident, or a child of divorce? Have you had to witness or even support someone close to you experiencing a tough time? Maybe you've gone through your fair share of sadness, but you have also been given tremendous advantages and opportunities that allowed you to enjoy positive experiences that you've always wished you could share. Allow yourself to be inspired by the roads you've traveled thus far in life.

REVIEWING YOUR SELF-ASSESSMENT

It can be hard to recognize just how much you have to offer without seeing it in black-and-white, which is why we tell you to make lists of your skills, hobbies, natural talents, and so forth. The other thing you can do is create a chart. Nothing is better for illuminating all the great things you have accomplished and matching them to potential nonprofits. We thought it would be helpful to share some examples.

1. Antonio is a full-time college student in Dallas, major-
   ing in mechanical engineering. He's held summer

jobs since he was sixteen but otherwise hasn't had any professional experience. The third-born of five siblings, he's used to having to work hard to get attention in his family and considers himself scrappy and self-sufficient. Recently, though, he was dealt an emotional blow when his good friend Matthew died of an overdose following a battle with depression.

Antonio's chart might look like this:

JOB SKILLS	HOBBIES	ACCESS	LIFE EXPERIENCE	NATURAL TALENTS
Supervising dogs at the Pampered Pet Kennel	Playing World of Warcraft	Aunt Arlene's vet clinic	Matt's death	Detail oriented
Assisting at Aunt Arlene's veterinary clinic	Cycling	Chemistry department lab	Not getting into first- or second-choice college	Good with math
	Playing pool		Winning first place in senior science fair	Decent Spanish

Based on his chart, Antonio might consider investigating these possibilities:*

---

* While the organizations listed are all real, we are using them as hypothetical examples. To inquire as to what opportunities really exist at any of these agencies, please go to their individual websites or give them a call.

Volunteer. Mentor a high-school team as they build a robot for BEST Robotics, Inc.; join the planning committee for the Dino Dash at the Museum of Nature and Science; advocate for the Texas Bicycle Coalition; coordinate Math Blazers competition for Girls and Boys Club.

Board Service. The Queenie Foundation, Inc. (supports animal protection).

Philanthropy. Humane Society; Mental Health America, Dallas; National Math and Science Initiative; Get-Well Gamers Foundation.

2. Shannon, a stay-at-home mother in Washington, DC, has just registered her youngest daughter for preschool. Before the twins were born she had a job with a marketing firm specializing in bars and restaurants, but after trying to juggle a full-time career with childrearing, she quit and hasn't worked in the years since. She dreams of opening her own coffee shop one day and selling the cinnamon rolls that everyone begs her to make for every bake sale and fund-raiser.

When she completes her self-assessment, her chart looks like this:

JOB SKILLS	HOBBIES	ACCESS	LIFE EXPERIENCE	NATURAL TALENTS
Five years of Web design	Baking	A minivan	Twins!	Making up stories, puppet shows, plays, etc.
Good computer skills	Playing the cello		Finishing the marathon	Patience
Still Internet savvy			Advocating for Dad at the nursing home	Can tell a good joke

Based on her chart, Shannon might consider these possibilities:

Volunteer. Cook for Food and Friends; donate baked goods to Parents/Family Café; be a tour guide for the Kennedy Center; deliver meals for Meals on Wheels.

Board Service. Washington Center for Aging Services.

Philanthropy. Used Book Café, whose profits go to Housing-Works; Nutra-Net, which teaches kids to cook nutritious meals; Resolve, the National Infertility Association; National Citizens' Coalition for Nursing Home Reform.

    3. A lot of professionals identify strongly with their careers, and Molly is one of them. When she was younger she

harbored fantasies of performing with a modern dance troupe. She has always been practical, however, and so became an accountant instead. She gave her job everything she had and is now a manager at a large accounting firm. Molly is proud of how quickly she has risen up the corporate ladder. Lately, though, she thought it might be a good idea to expand her social network.

When she completes her self-assessment, Molly's chart looks like this:

JOB SKILLS	HOBBIES	ACCESS	LIFE EXPERIENCE	NATURAL TALENTS
Budget analysis	Does Pilates count?	Computer	Performing solo on stage	Analytical mind
PC software applications		Tax and legal experts	Parachuting	Confident
Negotiation			Fending off that mugger	Persuasive

Based on her chart, Molly might consider the following possibilities:

Volunteer. Teach self-defense at Kidpower International; tutor GED candidates for Chrysalis, L.A.

Board Service. Dance Resource Center of Los Angeles; National Women's Martial Arts Federation.

Philanthropy. World Impact, L.A., a ministry that caters to the inner city; Friends Outside, which serves prison inmates, ex-offenders, and their families.

4. Charles, living in a suburb of Chicago, is a newly retired pharmacist looking forward to spending more time with his grandkids and playing with his band the Young at Hearts. He has thought about writing a memoir about his time spent as a World War II fighter pilot, but he's never quite sure how to begin. He's an avid poker player and loves heading to the casinos whenever his wife takes off for her "weekend with the girls."

Charles's self-assessment looks like this:

JOB SKILLS	HOBBIES	ACCESS	LIFE EXPERIENCE	NATURAL TALENTS
Expert chemist	Playing the piano for the Young at Hearts	Musical instruments	Piloting bombers	Excellent memory
Good manager	Writing and poetry		Thirty-three years of marriage to the same woman	Compassion
Patience with clients, especially the elderly who take a lot of meds	Poker		Raising a daughter with Down's syndrome	An aptitude for teaching

Charles's chart suggests he might look into the following nonprofits:

Volunteer. Play the piano at the Misericordia Home; sell tickets for the Easter Seals poker night fund-raiser.

Board Service. MedAccess Chicago; Rock for Kids.

Philanthropy. Council for Jewish Elderly; Veterans of Foreign Wars.

MANAGING EXPECTATIONS

As confident as we are that most people have more to offer to a nonprofit than they realize, we can't promise that the list of job skills, informal skills, and natural talents you put together will be enough to land you your dream position. As in any organization, the needs at a nonprofit vary widely, and for some opportunities, certain standards and requirements will be mandatory for applicants, such as a master's in social work or a valid driver's license, in order to be accepted. It doesn't make any sense for a nonprofit to assign someone who is "good with numbers" as board treasurer, however eagerly he wants the position, when there is another candidate available with CPA credentials. On the other hand, if that person who is good with numbers also happens to have experience in real estate, he could be extremely helpful in helping locate, negotiate for, and develop a site for the nonprofit's new headquarters.

NEXT STEPS

You know what you're good at, you know what you have to offer any nonprofit lucky enough to get you. Now what are you supposed to do with all this information? Well, you're not doing anyone any good, least of all yourself, by sitting on the gold mine of skills, talent, and good intentions you've uncovered. Now is your chance to turn those good intentions into effective, sustainable, personally fulfilling action. Next we'll explore the variety of roles available for anyone who wants to be a volunteer, serve on a board, donate money to a cause, or bring a spirit of idealism into his or her current workplace.

IDEALISM IN ACTION

I GREW UP IN A SMALL TOWN IN NORTHEASTERN IOWA. WHEN I WAS FIVE OR SIX, MY MOM ASKED ME TO HELP HER WITH A PROJECT. SHE WAS BAKING BANANA BREAD IN LITTLE LOAVES AND PACKAGING IT WITH RED AND GREEN CURLING RIBBON. IT WAS THE CHRISTMAS SEASON AND SHE WAS MAKING GIFTS TO SHARE WITH OUR NEIGHBORS AND FRIENDS. WE SET OUT ONE EVENING TO DELIVER THE CHRISTMAS GOODIES AND ARRIVED AT THE HOME OF AN ELDERLY NEIGHBOR. WHEN WE RANG HER DOORBELL, WE HEARD HER CRY OUT, ASKING FOR HELP. MOM TRIED THE DOOR, AND IT WAS THANKFULLY UNLOCKED. WE WENT IN AND FOUND THAT OUR NEIGHBOR HAD FALLEN EARLIER IN THE DAY AND HAD BROKEN HER HIP. SHE COULD

NOT GET UP, SHE LIVED ALONE, SHE COULD NOT REACH THE PHONE, AND SHE WAS NOT EXPECTING ANY VISITORS. WE CALLED FOR HELP, SHE WAS TAKEN TO THE HOSPITAL, AND SHE HEALED COMPLETELY. SHE MIGHT NOT HAVE IF MY MOTHER HAD DECIDED NOT TO BE NEIGHBORLY, AND IF SHE HAD NOT WANTED TO TEACH ME ABOUT BEING NEIGHBORLY. THIS INCI-DENT REMAINS A VERY POWERFUL STORY IN MY LIFE. A SIMPLE LOAF OF BANANA BREAD, A NEIGHBOR, A CRISIS, ALL UNITED BY AN ACT OF SERVICE.

—Valerie Jones, volunteer, the Minnesota Association for Volunteer Administration, COVAA/ALIVE (Association for Leaders in Volunteer Engagement), Celeste's Dream Community Garden, the Greater Twin Cities United Way Cultural Dynamics Committee, the Career Services Department of College of St. Benedict; Roseville, Minnesota

PART II

Taking Action

5

Everything You Need to Know About Volunteering

When I am going through a hard time, or even a hard day, volunteering and helping someone else can swing my mood to the positive in no time. In fact, I have started telling people going through a hard time to go volunteer. It will make you feel better and take your mind off your struggles, or at least put your struggles in perspective.

—KATHY MORELAND, VOLUNTEER, SENIOR RESOURCES

(AKA MEALS ON WHEELS); COLUMBIA, SOUTH CAROLINA

SO MANY CHOICES

If there's one thing we've reiterated throughout this book, it's that there's no one-size-fits-all way of changing the world for the better. The same goes for volunteering. In fact, there are about ten different types of volunteerism, each unique in the way it will engage you, from the one-shot convenience of hit-and-run volunteering, to the social opportunities of group volunteering, to the excitement of voluntourism. The great thing about all these kinds of volunteerism is that, like a well-varied wardrobe, you can mix and match to suit your needs. You outgrow a project or position? Try a new one on for size. Your schedule shrinks? There's something less time-consuming out there for you, maybe even within the same nonprofit. Can't decide between two perfect fits? Give them each a little test run. Who knows, maybe with some creativity you can combine the two into a one-of-a-kind opportunity. It's all in your hands.

As always, your needs and expectations are two of the most important things to consider when deciding how you want to volunteer. We have categorized the various types of volunteering under the following four priorities or motivating factors that most often guide an individual to donate his or her time to an organization: flexibility, a chance to participate in social activities, a need for experience, and a desire to make the most of one's skills. Not only should this arrangement help you quickly identify which type will best suit your needs, but it also reveals how various volunteer opportunities fit into several overlapping categories. Once you've read the chapter, check out the more than fifteen thousand volunteer opportunities posted on the Idealist.org website to see who is looking for someone like you right this minute.

IF YOU WANT FLEXIBILITY

Hit-and-Run Volunteering

Perfect for someone who wants to inject his day with a feel-good boost, hit-and-run volunteering is like a shot of Red Bull for the soul. Also known as "episodic volunteering," this is an excellent opportunity for the person who doesn't have much time to spare. Rather than commit to one cause, or one organization, people who practice hit-and-run volunteering seek out individual projects that require little time and no training yet where they can provide much-needed help. Many people fulfill their desire to serve their community in this way. In fact, one of our staff, Erin, does it all the time. "I'm passionate about several causes, and there's no way I could give enough time to all of them. This way, when I see I have two hours free on the weekend, I can do something like help box groceries at a local food bank and know that I was able to lend a hand." There's no reason to feel bad if episodic volunteering is the only thing you can squeeze into your busy life; even the most passionate supporters of the nonprofit world have a hard time fitting it in!

ADVANTAGES
- Great for infusing variety into your routine
- A good way to give an organization a test run if you're researching longer-term volunteer opportunities
- Allows you to avoid the burnout that can happen when volunteers spread themselves too thin or become consumed by a project or cause

Getting Started. To find hit-and-run projects, check out your local volunteer center's website.

In addition to listings on Idealist.org, you can find a directory of volunteer centers on the Points of Light & Hands On Network website—www.pointsoflight.org—or call 1-800-Volunteer.

Your local center often will post a calendar announcing volunteer opportunities throughout the month. In late winter, for example, there may be posts asking for volunteers to spend a Saturday teaching families how to properly prepare their tax forms and claim their rightful tax deductions and credits (a perfect one-shot opportunity for a CPA or financial planner). A shelter might be searching for someone to read bedtime stories to their preschoolers for an hour. Or maybe the organizers of a fun run will need individuals to help with crowd control for a few hours during the race. There are also programs specifically geared toward episodic volunteering, such as RSVP (www.seniorcorps.org/about/programs/rsvp.asp), which caters to volunteers over the age of fifty-five. The variety inherent in hit-and-run volunteering makes it one of the most pleasurable and sustainable ways to contribute to your community.

Online Volunteering

You may see some nonprofits refer to this form of contributing time as virtual volunteering, but there's nothing virtual about it. From your kitchen table at home, armed with a computer, you can make as effective and important a contribution as anything you could do by walking through a nonprofit's doors. It's a great option for people with strong writing, design, or tech skills, and projects run the gamut of complexity and sophistication. Online volunteers can design websites, logos, and branding materials; write grant proposals; organize digital photos; even act as a clipping service, searching the web and collecting any mention of the group in the media.

ADVANTAGES

- A terrific option for anyone with limited transportation, time, or physical mobility
- An opportunity to help an organization that may not have an office in your area or that serves a national or global need
- Flexible hours

Getting Started. You'll likely find many opportunities listed on any nonprofit's website or in a volunteer center database. You could also approach an organization you like with suggested projects based on your particular area of expertise or interest. For example:

- Web communication, such as creating discussion forums, blogs, or podcasts
- Web and technical maintenance
- Advocacy and fund-raising, such as creating a campaign or working on branding materials
- Research
- Offering professional advice, such as reviewing strategic or business plans
- Writing text for website or brochures
- Grant writing
- Database management
- Proofreading and editing
- Translation

Days of Service

Many cities and organizations, often in tandem with each other or with companies, have designated certain days, weeks, months, and holidays as particularly apropos for encouraging civic engagement. For example, Martin Luther King Day is a big citywide service opportunity in many parts of the country, a day in which nonprofits organize people to come together to complete projects that further the ideals promoted by the civil rights activist. Other nationally recognized days and weeks of service include:

JANUARY

National Mentoring Month: www.whomentoredyou.org
Martin Luther King Jr. Day of Service: www.mlkday.org

FEBRUARY

Groundhog Job Shadow Day: www.jobshadow.org
Random Acts of Kindness Week:
www.actsofkindness.org/people/days.asp

MARCH

Read Across America: www.nea.org/readacross
Cesar Chavez Day of Service and Learning:
www.chavezfoundation.org

APRIL

International Children's Book Day: www.ibby.org
National Youth Service Day: www.ysa.org/nysd
Global Youth Service Day: www.gysd.net
National Volunteer Week:
  www.pointsoflight.org/programs/seasons/nvw
Earth Day: www.earthday.gov
World Book Day: www.unesco.org/culture/bookday

MAY

Older Americans Month: www.aoa.gov/press/oam/oam.asp
Join Hands Day: www.joinhandsday.org

JULY

National Summer Learning Day: www.summerlearning.org

AUGUST

National Night Out: www.nationaltownwatch.org/nno
Community Build Day: www.fsround.org/community/cbd.htm

SEPTEMBER

National Neighborhood Day: www.neighborhoodday.org
National Public Lands Day: www.npld.com
My Good Deed, September 11: www.mygooddeed.org

Intergeneration Day: www.intergenerationday.org
Make a Difference Day: www.makeadifferenceday.com
Kids Care Week: www.kidscare.org/about/kidscareweek
Be the Change Day: www.saalt.org/bethechange.php

NOVEMBER————————————————————————

Youth Appreciation Week:
www.optimist.org/default.cfm?content=members/mbrcdpa10.html
National Family Volunteer Day:
www.pointsoflight.org/programs/seasons/nfvd
National Family Week: www.nationalfamilyweek.org

DECEMBER————————————————————————

International Volunteer Day:
www.worldvolunteerweb.org/int-l-volunteer-day.html

We should probably list Thanksgiving as an unofficial day of service, since nonprofits receive the most phone calls from prospective volunteers on the days preceding it and even on the day itself. It's understandable that we would want to reach out to others on a day that encourages us to count our blessings. However, while you always deserve kudos for good intentions, we'd like to suggest that the next time you're inspired to volunteer on Thanksgiving, hold on to the thought but hold off on picking up the phone. Most nonprofits have more volunteers on Thanksgiving than they can handle, but are desperate for more hands every other time of the year. If you do decide to volunteer on Thanksgiving, make sure to call organizations several weeks in advance, and don't be discouraged if you're turned away. Rather, eat your turkey, start your holiday shopping, and give that nonprofit another ring on Monday. They'll be delighted to hear from you.

ADVANTAGES
- An opportunity to get involved with a variety of groups and causes
- Low commitment, high emotional ROI
- Projects tend to be ones which can be completed quickly; therefore volunteers see the immediate fruits of their labor
- An excellent rallying point when coordinating a volunteer activity with colleagues or friends.

Getting Started. It's so easy. Simply go to any of the websites listed above or check out any volunteer center or network's list of community service days, such as:

Point of Light & Hands On Network:
   www.pointsoflight.org/programs/seasons
Learn and Serve Clearinghouse:
   www.servicelearning.org/instant_info/links
Corporation for National and Community Service:
   www.nationalserviceresources.org/link/category/30

IF YOU WANT SOCIAL ACTIVITIES

Group Volunteering

In our zeal to make a difference, change the world, ease our collective guilt—whatever motivates us to donate our time—it's easy to forget that volunteering isn't just about "doing good." It's also about having fun. And sometimes, the *only* reason to do a volunteer project is because it's fun. So why not make a social activity out of it and invite a group of friends or colleagues to join you in a volunteer project? Hand out wristbands at a music festival (and of course stick around for the show), train together for a charity run, or offer to paint faces and serve snacks at a community center Halloween party before heading out for your own fright night revelry.

Here's another idea—make your next date a volunteer project. You could help kids at the children's museum make gingerbread houses, take some dogs at the local shelter out for a walk, or make Valentine's Day cards to hand out at a senior citizen's center. You'll participate in a shared activity that will tell you a lot more about your date and give you more to talk about later at dinner than if you spent two hours sitting side by side in a movie theater.

And if you don't have a date, volunteering might be a way to get one. If you love modern art, why not become a docent at a museum where you can meet other people who share your passion? Also, almost every city has one or more volunteer groups that have been formed specifically for singles who want to do good work while meeting other singles with similar interests and values. Some nationally known organizations are:

Single Volunteers: www.singlevolunteers.org
Singles for Charities: www.singlesforcharities.com
Planet Earth Singles: www.planetearthsingles.com

> You can also go to www.idealist.org and search "Singles" for a list of nonprofit organizations and volunteer opportunities currently available in your area.

ADVANTAGES
- Easy, low-pressure activities
- Great morale- and team-building opportunities
- Perfect way for someone new in town to make friends and get to know his or her community

Getting Started. Sometimes people want someone to get them over their inertia, so they're happy for you to lead and set up the activity, time, and place so all they have to do is show up. But if you're trying to get to know people, you can use the project selection as a way to gauge their interests and skills. Involving your group in deciding where to volunteer will also improve the chances that everyone has a good time and feels accomplished at the end of the day. Ultimately, of course, someone will have to take responsibility for setting up the project logistics and coordinating with the chosen organization's project manager.

Again, when you're looking for service opportunities, your local volunteer center will likely have a long list of possible choices to choose from. You could also page through local magazines where organizations will place ads announcing upcoming events and even calls for volunteers. Don't forget to ask the members of your group whether one of them is already connected to a nonprofit. They may jump at the chance to share this part of their life with you. You can also search by group on Idealist.org's advanced search for volunteer opportunities.

Family Volunteering

Maybe you would love to donate your time to a cause but don't because you lack child care or want to reserve your free time for your family. The good news is that there are many volunteer projects perfectly suited for people of all ages that can serve as a wonderful bonding opportunity for an entire family. They also provide an excellent opportunity to pass valuable examples of compassion, empathy, sharing, and giving on to children. If you're looking for a way to bring the kids along, parks, senior citizen centers, zoos, and recreation departments are all great places to look for family-friendly activities. Painting over graffiti, doing landscaping, freshening up the local school grounds, planting a community garden—kids love that stuff. They get outside, they get dirty, they burn off energy, and it sure beats another round of mini-golf.

- Can offer a unique way to learn something new and bond with a partner or spouse
- Fits built-in family time into busy schedules
- Presents an opportunity to teach kids the value in reaching out to serve others
- Often provides a chance to get involved with a community other than one's own

Getting Started. You can always go to your local volunteer center, which will list one-day events, many of which will need groups for walks, festivals, and fairs. In addition, many local parenting magazines print lists of volunteer opportunities. You might also contact your community Parks and Recreation Department, which is often looking for extra help with special projects. In addition, you could look online for opportunities. Simply typing "family-friendly volunteering" and the name of your city into any search engine will probably present you with a list of possibilities. Or try:

The Volunteer Family: www.volunteersolutions.org/vfamily/volunteer
Doing Good Together: www.doinggoodtogether.org
Family Cares: www.familycares.org
Generations United: www.gu.org

> Check out www.idealist.org/kt/familyvolunteer.html for a comprehensive list of family-friendly volunteer local and national resources.

IF YOU WANT EXPERIENCE

Internships

For many, internships are the best way to get a foot in the door of the career or organization where they hope to work someday. Even though we're used to thinking of unpaid internships in terms of career-path stepping stones, they are indeed a form of volunteering, albeit one that offers an increased opportunity to do more challenging work than the typical volunteer experience, and one that carries more weight on a resume. Ideally, interns also receive the attention of a mentor or supervisor and access to all that person's wisdom and experience, someone who will also be willing to write a letter of recommendation on the intern's behalf. For someone who likes structure and consistency, or projects with a set beginning and end date, internships are often great ways to contribute to a nonprofit while also building professional skills and networking.

ADVANTAGES
- Offers a detailed sneak peek at the inner workings of an organization
- Allows you to get a feel for a job or field before committing to it full-time
- Excellent networking opportunity
- Great resume builder

Getting Started. Many organizations will list internship opportunities on their websites. But if they don't, you might be able to create one. Ask for an informational interview with the head of the group or department that interests you and explain that you'd like to offer them your time in exchange for the opportunity to work side by side with someone willing to share his or her insight and experience with you. Alternatively, Idealist.org is an excellent resource: www.idealist .org/if/idealist/en/advancedsearch/internship/default.

Term of Service

Engaging in a term of service generally requires you to commit yourself full-time for at least one year, sometimes two, to a nonprofit organization that will train you to provide service to a community or cause. You've probably heard of some of the most well-known year-of-service programs—Teach for America, Peace Corps, AmeriCorps. There is a huge variety to choose from, and all have different expectations of their members. Many require a college degree, but not all. AmeriCorps, for example, doesn't require a degree for all of its programs, and Citiyear is geared toward people coming right out of school.

The most important thing to keep in mind when considering a term of service is that it's equivalent to accepting a full-time job, and a low-paying job at that. You must be able to afford to live on the limited stipend the program offers (some also offer minimal child-care benefits). For some, this is too much of a sacrifice; for others, it actually enhances the volunteer experience by helping them to fully comprehend the financial realities of the communities they are serving. Programs also give out education awards, funds that are allocated to further a volunteer's schooling or pay off student loans, or they may receive an end-of-service stipend.

Participating in a term-of-service program can be a life-changing experience. It can also be a career booster. It's possible that the work you do during your one or two years of service will be far more demanding and require much more responsibility than an entry-level position with any other organization, whether nonprofit or for-profit. But even if you wind up doing a more task-oriented job after your term of service, you'll still walk away with excellent experience. For example, join Teach for America, and you're running your own classroom. (That's not to say that every project will be so hands-on with the community; some term-of-service programs are very direct-service oriented, and some are indirect, focusing on capacity building or fund-raising rather than direct client work.)

In addition, people who already have management experience might consider a term-of-service program if they're considering a career switch. If you're currently a corporate banker but think you might like to become a program manager for a nonprofit, a year of service will give you a realistic sense of what such a change would entail, and give you a chance to see if it's something you really want to do.

Overall, term-of-service volunteering is an excellent entry into the nonprofit sector no matter what stage you're at in life, whether reevaluating your priorities, switching careers, just starting out, or thinking of retiring. (SeniorCorps and ExperienceCorps are geared specifically for people over the age of fifty-five.)

ADVANTAGES
- Can jump-start a career because participants take on more responsibility than in most traditional for-profit entry-level positions
- Offers possible career-switchers a trial period for gauging their readiness to make the leap from the for-profit sector
- Provides unparalleled insight into the needs and circumstances of the community being served
- Introduces an opportunity to earn funds for higher education while garnering real on-the-ground experience

Getting Started. You'll first want to determine whether you'll realistically be able to commit to a long-term project. Questions to consider are:

- Are you willing to relocate?
- Can you afford to take a leave of absence from your school or work?
- Will you be able to ask people at home to handle things while you are gone? (Pets, bills, home maintenance, etc.)
- Are you prepared to live in conditions that might be significantly poorer than your own?

To explore term-of-service opportunities, try the following websites:

Public Allies: www.publicallies.org
Jesuit Volunteer Corps: www.jesuitvolunteers.org

Camphill: www.camphill.org

Art Corps: www.artcorp.org

Teach for America: www.teachforamerica.org

AmeriCorps: www.americorps.org

SeniorCorps www.seniorcorps.org

AmeriCorps Vista:
www.americorps.org/for_individuals/choose/vista.asp

International Volunteering

There are volunteer opportunities all over the world, and if you've got an adventurous spirit, transporting your energy, enthusiasm, knowledge, skills, and good intentions to another country can be the opportunity of a lifetime.

Many people assume that unless you can take off for six months or a year, international volunteerism isn't an option. Yes, you'll get a deeper cross-cultural experience the longer you stay in a foreign country, but a person can also get a lot of good done in a week. Think of yourself as an important link in a chain—every volunteer's time and effort builds on the one before, making the chain longer and stronger so it can reach that much further.

> The approach to organizing and overseeing nonprofits varies widely throughout the world, as do individual countries' systems for setting up, registering, and regulating nonprofits. It is beyond the scope of this book to try to document those systems. You can, however, go to

DANIEL, MINERVA

Thu Feb 09 2017

The Idealist.org handbook to

33029068011972

Hold note:

*

*

*

*

*

*

*

*

the Idealist.org website (and the Nonprofit FAQ) at www.idealist.org/ tools/support-orgs.html for a list of centers that support nonprofits in other countries. The International Center for Nonprofit Law (www .icnl.org) and the Center for Civil Society at Johns Hopkins University (www.jhu.edu/~ccss) also offer information and analysis about the climate for nonprofits in many countries of the world.

There are two kinds of projects that generally need international volunteers: developmental and environmental. Developmental projects are human- or community-focused, revolving around health, nutrition, education, the economy, sustainability, and infrastructure (such as building wells). Environmental projects are conservation- or environment-based. They can entail typical cleanup endeavors, but also include projects like tagging sea turtles or counting bald eagles around breeding time.

ADVANTAGES
- An opportunity to experience a true cross-cultural exchange
- Development of foreign-language skills
- The chance to act as an ambassador for your country

Getting Started. You can go about international volunteering either on your own or through a program. The first option can be the experience of a lifetime; independent traveling and volunteering is ideal for people who want to set their own itinerary and shape their own donor experience. To plan such an adventure, you'd of course use online resources—Idealist.org is a good place to start—but before your trip, you might also contact an organization you already know to see if they have international offices or partners in the countries you hope to visit. That way you'll already have a point of reference when you arrive at your destination. Also, if you work for a multinational corporation, it's possible they have resources set up for employees transferring to other countries that include lists of service organizations. See if they're willing to share those lists with you.

The downside to traveling and volunteering independently is that you'll have no safety net. Without any effective screening mechanisms in place, you can wind up in Bangladesh or Ankara thinking you've got a place to stay or at least an interesting project to join, only to learn that in fact you are responsible for finding your own lodging, or the project has folded. In extreme cases you can also discover that the organization you thought you'd like to contribute to is a fly-by-night operation that either engages in unethical practices or has simply misrepresented their capacity to handle volunteers.

And of course, before you get on that airplane, learn about the country and the community you're heading to—the history and politics, the cultural expectations, the preferred dress, and traditional foods.

Having a basic grasp of the language is extremely helpful—it will make your travels easier and save someone at the organization from having to translate everything for you. This will ensure that even a short trip is a productive experience. One of the main advantages of volunteering through an international program is that they specifically work with English speakers and will make sure that you are placed in an environment where you'll be able to get work done without being a burden to anyone.

You'll also want to think carefully about the reality of traveling in certain countries on your own. If you are a woman traveling alone, it may be harder to have a positive experience in certain areas than in others. The same goes for people of color or alternative sexual orientation. Even the mere fact that you are an American should factor into your decision of where to travel and volunteer alone. Other countries have strong opinions about us, good and bad. That's not to say that if you're a woman or Latino or wear an American lapel pin that you're automatically going to be a target for harassment or a political diatribe, but you must recognize that without the protection of an established group, you may be at greater risk for some uncomfortable confrontations. We suggest that you be emotionally prepared should you decide to travel independently in a culturally conservative or politically volatile country.

If partaking in an independent volunteer experience sounds risky, you might prefer to participate in a formal international volunteer program. There are many programs run by both nonprofits and for-profits that take care of all the logistics necessary for a safe and productive volunteer experience. Some organizations will pay for all of your expenses. Most, however, in exchange for a fee, will arrange your housing, your meals, and the particular project in which you'll be involved. You don't need to have any particular skill set or knowledge to participate in these groups—they're great at finding opportunities for anyone who wants to join in. Granted, you won't have the schedule flexibility you might have had were you traveling alone, but the peace of mind and planning help might be worth sacrificing a little spontaneity.

The following groups do not charge a fee:

UN Volunteers: www.unvolunteers.org
Catholic Network of Volunteers: www.cnvs.org
Peace Corps: www.peacecorps.gov
CHF International Visiting International Professionals Program: www.chfinternational.org/vip_program
International Executive Service Corps: www.iesc.org
Jewish Coalition for Service: www.jewishservice.org
Voluntary Service Overseas: www.vsocan.org
World Wide Opportunities on Organic Farms: www.wwoof.org

When doing your research (Idealist.org has an extensive directory, as does Transitions Abroad, www.transitionsabroad .com), find other people who have recently returned from a stint with the organization. Ask them for an honest assessment of what they liked and didn't like about the program and their experience.

More organizations to check out:

International Volunteer Programs Association: www.volunteerinternational.org
International Health Volunteers: http://internationalhealthvolunteers.org
Universal Giving: www.universalgiving.org/jsp/volunteer/index.do
Voluntary Service Overseas: www.vsocan.org

Whether traveling on your own or with a program, you'll want to learn everything you can about the nonprofits you intend to work with. Use the Web—Google articles or press clippings, go to the organization's website, find blogs to hear what people are saying about the agency—talk to friends, coworkers, people at church, anyone with a connection to the issue or group you're researching. Is the organization already affiliated with one that you know? Knowing that a local nonprofit in faraway Ukraine is connected to the Red Cross or Red Crescent might help lend it a sense of familiarity and legitimacy that will put your mind at ease before you embark on your journey.

Another secure way to volunteer internationally is through a faith-based group, many of which are doing some of the hardest development work in the world. Keep in mind that many religious or faith-based groups do not proselytize; they may simply have a faith-based charter, so don't immediately write them off if you're not religious or comfortable promoting or participating in a particular faith.

Some faith-based groups you might explore:

American Friends Service Committee: www.afsc.org
American Jewish World Service: www.ajws.org
Catholic Network of Volunteer Service:
www.cnvs.org/aboutus/index.php

Voluntourism

What if the only time you have to get away from your routine is when you take vacation? More and more people are seeking to enrich their vacation or business trip plans with volunteer projects. The voluntourism trend has grown so much, in fact, that there's an entire niche in the travel industry dedicated to helping you make arrangements for a comfy hotel bed (although many vacation planners cater to travelers willing to rough it) in which to relax after a day of building homes, reading with orphans, or cleaning up coral reefs. In this way, individuals can combine their passion for travel and cultural exchange with their zeal for making a difference wherever they go. And many times, they'll come back tanner and wiser.

ADVANTAGES
- Satisfies the need for a change of pace or scenery while also contributing more than tourist dollars
- Great option for time-starved vacationers who wish they could volunteer
- Offers a less intense volunteer experience, sometimes with more comfortable amenities, than a traditional international volunteer program

Getting Started. If you're interested in finding a great voluntourism organization, visit:

Voluntourism.org: www.Voluntourism.org
The Travel Abroad section of the **Transitions Abroad** website: www.transitionsabroad.com/listings/travel

IF YOU WANT TO EXPAND THE REACH OF YOUR TALENTS OR SKILLS

Skilled Volunteering

In Chapter 1 we talked a bit about skilled volunteerism as a way to contribute your professional expertise or other specific knowledge to a nonprofit. It's a slightly different kind of volunteer contribution because some nonprofits will have to think more strategically about where someone like you would be most effective, as opposed to putting you to work wherever they need a pair of hands.

> While you can be a skilled volunteer without the level of commitment involved in board service, and you can serve on a board without specific skills, there is no doubt that board service is an excellent opportunity to apply your professional knowledge. For this reason, we'll postpone our discussion of the particulars of board service for a more detailed one in Chapter 6.

There are, however, many ways in which someone with special professional skills can make significant contributions to a community. For example, optometrists and eye specialists can volunteer with Unite for Sight; every city has a network of organizations looking for lawyers willing to donate some time and expertise; Accountants Without Borders arranges similar opportunities for finance professionals; Geekcorps sends technology experts to teach individuals and businesses in developing countries how to improve their digital and communications capacities; teachers who can tutor individuals in literature and writing, social studies, math, or science for the GED, or in English as a second language (ESL), are in high demand at community centers across the country.

You might also consider government-supported groups such as the Peace Corps. Unlike some term-of-service groups, these organizations do look for participants with certain skills and knowledge, since they are often deeply involved in building communities. Keep in mind that while these groups will pay your travel and living expenses, in exchange they generally expect you to commit to a minimum of one year of service.

The following are organizations that look for skilled volunteers:

CitizenCorps: www.citizencorps.gov
Peace Corps: www.peacecorps.gov
Geekcorps: www.geekcorps.org
Architecture for Humanity: www.architectureforhumanity.org
Engineers Without Borders: www.ewb-usa.org/index.php
International Health Volunteers:
   www.internationalhealthvolunteers.org
Clearinghouse for Volunteer Accounting Services:
   www.cvas-usa.org

ADVANTAGES
- Excellent professional networking opportunity.
- The chance to earn respect and even admiration from others who don't have your specialty

- An opportunity to do more significant work than some volunteer positions will allow

Getting Started. Some professions have national organizations devoted to connecting skilled individuals with groups who need them. For example, cosmetologists can go to www .lookgoodfeelbetter.org/audience/volunteers/apply. If you can't find a directory specific to your field, contacting a professional association might be a good place to start.

Do-It-Yourself Volunteering

Sometimes you just can't find the perfect volunteer opportunity; nothing grabs your interest, or the nonprofit you approach isn't sure how to use you quite yet. If this happens, the best option may be to develop your own project. Organizations often don't know what they don't know, so why not be the one to bring them up to speed? Other times, they know what they need but don't have the capacity to make it happen. Why not get them started? Propose a way to modernize their data-collecting process, enhance their online visibility, or spruce up their marketing materials. Not only will the organization be impressed with your contribution, they'll remember your initiative, which could come in handy should you be interested in taking on a bigger role or tapping networking opportunities later down the road.

- Tailoring your volunteer experience to your particular interests
- Setting your own schedule
- The opportunity to bring the organization something they otherwise would never have known they needed

Getting Started. In general, the best DIY projects are ones that enhance visibility for the organization. If you notice that a group isn't using technology to its advantage, propose writing a blog or creating a podcast. Give new tone and energy to their website with a refreshed web design. Outreach projects, too, can improve community support and participation with the group without taxing their resources.

> **Many of the options listed in the Online Volunteering section on page 78 are also excellent DIY projects.**

Most of the time we recommend you direct your inquiries to an organization's volunteer manager, but if you're doing a DIY project, you might pitch your plans straight to the appropriate staff person in charge of the area relevant to your idea. Ask if you can add a column to the newsletter, or offer to set up informal lectures or seminars at the local college campus. Be careful, though, not to get too ambitious. You may have some terrific programs in mind that would boost revenue or increase community participation, but until the nonprofit gets to know you it's going to be hard for them to entrust you with true leadership positions. Bide your time, build trust, and perhaps later the nonprofit will be open to your suggestions for a larger initiative. And don't get discouraged should the organization you approach turn you down. They may agree that your program is valuable but just not be in a position to implement or support your idea. If that's the case, try another organization.

DO WHAT YOU SAY YOU'LL DO

It's not easy being a volunteer manager. They're constantly recruiting new volunteers while organizing and placing the ones they've already got on hand; they're the ones who have to scramble to find a replacement volunteer should someone not show up. If you commit to volunteer for an organization, remember that if you don't uphold that commitment, you will be making the volunteer manager's life a lot harder. Also, remember that your actions will likely affect the individuals or groups who are served by the nonprofit. If you agree to mentor a child and back out, you're letting that child down, that child's family down, and the volunteer manager who now has to explain why you aren't going to show up.

AT A GLANCE

As we mentioned, though we have categorized these types of volunteerism into overarching categories, there are many ways in which the types of service contributions mentioned in this chapter can overlap in terms of how they meet your particular needs, depending on the project. For example, an accountant who volunteers for one day instructing low-income families how to properly complete their tax forms is doing a hit-and-run project while also gaining experience and expanding the reach of his professional skills. The following chart illustrates these overlaps:

	FLEXIBILITY	SOCIAL ACTIVITIES	EXPERIENCE	SKILL EXPANSION
Hit-and-run	X	X	X	
Online	X		X	X
Days of Service	X	X		
Group		X		
Family		X		
Internship	X		X	X
Term of Service			X	X
International			X	X
Voluntourism		X	X	X
Skilled	X		X	X
DIY	X	X	X	X

The extraordinary fluidity and dynamism inherent in the volunteer experience can make it an extremely rewarding and exciting way to get involved in making the world a better place.

My interest in student activism, civil rights, and social justice issues brought me to apply for an Alternative Spring Break trip during my freshman year of college. Before being selected to work with Habitat for Humanity in rural Mississippi, I hadn't known much about the organization. That one week was one of the most influential experiences of my life. Upon my group's arrival, we were approached by a man who informed us that he represented the KKK and they were not happy that we were in town helping to house families that they thought were unworthy. It was inspiring for me to see the local volunteers—and my group—not shrink in the face of his threats, but work harder to accomplish our goal. Several years later I had the opportunity to revisit that community and I was overjoyed to see it thriving and continuing to grow.

—Alynn Woodson, director of volunteer engagement, Habitat for Humanity International; Americus, Georgia

6

Everything You Need to Know About Board Service

Consider these five people. Marina, a senior VP at an investment firm, believes that women facing retirement after years of building a career need support when creating the next chapter in their lives. Jake just got back from a year backpacking around the world after completing his degree in chemical engineering. Alan is a podiatrist with strong ties to his church. Leonora's mother was a foster grandmother, and now that her children are grown she is one, too. Emma, a grant writer and consultant, wants to ensure the future of her son's French-immersion preschool. A corporate executive, a recent graduate, a doctor, a stay-at-home mother, a consultant. None of these individuals have anything in common except that they each play a unique and vital role in their respective nonprofit organizations: they are board members.

Too often, when people think about what kind of person serves on a board, images of corporate executives or bejeweled women in pink Chanel suits come to mind. Board membership, many believe, is for the rich and the well connected, or for people who don't have real jobs and while away their days planning parties and black-tie functions. The truth is, however, that most board members and boards don't look the same, and the majority are populated by a hodgepodge of individuals from various backgrounds. The main prerequisite for any board member is that he or she care deeply about the welfare and long-term future of the organization. In Chapter 1, we talked about how board members invest their time and expertise in a nonprofit, but they also invest their hearts.

So who can join a board? What do you have to do? How does it benefit you? We'll answer all those questions and more in this chapter.

WHAT DOES THE BOARD DO?

Every independent nonprofit is guided by a board, a group of individuals who periodically gather to discuss the progress of the nonprofit and make the organization's financial and strategic decisions. It is a volunteer position, yet regardless of the unpaid nature of the work, these individuals are considered the nonprofit's legal guardians and governing body, obligated to make the best decisions possible regarding the assets and well-being of that organization.

Primarily, the board upholds the nonprofit's mission. Sometimes it even writes it. It is also responsible for hiring people for some of the higher-level jobs at the organization, such as the executive director. It may establish program goals and assess that program's performance. It will assess its own performance in upholding the vision and mission of the organization, setting realistic budgets and financial plans, and helping build the nonprofit's effectiveness and efficiency. The board also makes less broad decisions, such as whether to serve alcohol at fundraisers, or whether to accept funding from companies whose activities conflict with their values (e.g., a cancer support group accepting money from a cigarette company). It will decide what kind of health insurance to offer employees, and determine if or when it's time to replace the executive director.

Just as the size and structure of a nonprofit affect its organizational culture, they also affect the board's activities. Small and/or emerging organizations may require relatively loose standards and some hands-on participation from their board, whereas larger and/or established ones will likely have stricter rules and requirements in place and probably less opportunity for direct service or active involvement by the board in the organization's day-to-day activities.

AM I QUALIFIED?

There are two ways to join a board: you can apply, or you can be recruited. It's common, though, for people to react with "Who, me?" when either option is suggested. With the exception of people interested in board membership to further their careers (more on that later), it takes self-awareness and confidence to recognize one's value to a board. It's easy to get intimidated.

To ease your fears, we want to dispel two myths surrounding the requirements for board membership. The first is that all board members are the aforementioned socialites or white-collar executives. There's no doubt, of course, that people with years in their field and strong professional expertise can be of invaluable service to a nonprofit. If you've built up an extensive knowledge base or a network of personal and professional contacts, you have an unparalleled opportunity to spin them into gold for the right nonprofit in terms of access to information, fresh funding sources, and general assistance.

That said, board members by definition do not have to be people who have already climbed high up the professional ladder, and marketers, designers, lawyers, and accountants are certainly not the only professions that have relevance to a board's effectiveness. Boards need experts to handle various legal matters and financial details, but there are other activities, such as consulting, networking, and communicating with the media, that keep a nonprofit solvent, growing, and in the public eye.

> When the boys were in high school, I relaunched my life. I met a woman working with Ballet Hispanico that served Hispanic children in our New York neighborhood. I had had no experience in ballet other than having been forced to take ballet lessons as a child. I mean, I had been to the ballet. It was crazy! They weren't recruiting me as an artist, however, but for my management experience.
>
> —Janet Thompson, former board member of Ballet Hispanico, current board member of the Nonprofit Finance Fund; New York, New York

Boards often recruit individuals from any number of fields, including but not limited to government, business, PR, design, human resources, management, activism, law, medicine, tech, entrepreneurship, marketing, writing, event planning, fundraising, education, social work, real estate, media, finance, athletics, child care, and fine arts.

In other words, an effective board taps into the same kind of skills—including the informal knowledge and natural talents that we explored in Chapter 4—you use to help keep the place where you might currently work running at maximum speed and profitability.

Keep in mind, too, that if you are a member of the community served by the nonprofit, or if you have direct experience with the issue for which they are advocating or the problem they are trying to solve, your input could be invaluable to a board. What better way for them to know whether their plans and programs are having the desired effect than to hear from someone who lives with the consequences of their efforts every day? Some boards even establish requirements to ensure that they don't lose sight of the needs of their constituency. For example, an agency that serves the youth of their community may demand that at least two board seats be reserved for members under the age of eighteen. This ensures that someone representing the demographic the group aims to help has a chance to weigh in on any plans or decisions made by the board. Many organizations that cater to college students, too, will expect at least one student to be on the board to provide perspective.

The second myth, the one that spawns visions of Chanel suits, is that only wealthy or famous people need apply for board memberships. Some boards are specifically fund-raising boards, in which case, yes, they're going to be looking for someone with deep pockets and connections to others with deep pockets. The Boys and Girls Club may want a popular athlete or two on their board, for example, because those names on the letterhead will draw attention and look impressive. The athletes will be there to bring in generous donations, not to serve punch at the fund-raiser. If you fall into the category of individuals who can comfortably serve on that kind of board, terrific. If not, don't dismiss the idea that board membership is within your reach.

While it doesn't hurt for a board to have members with a lot of money and an in-depth understanding of marketing and media, boards are also looking for members who know people. That doesn't mean you have to be a socialite to be a desirable board member. It simply means that considering how dependent nonprofits are on donations, it's understandable that they are eager to have members with wide-reaching social and professional networks. So let's say you're interested in a local organization, and you've lived and worked in town for more than thirty years. You have a vested interest in the community, you know a large number of people (and hopefully are willing to speak to them about donating to the organization), and you may even have a good grasp of local politics and history. If you are as passionate about the issues as the current board members, and maybe even willing to serve punch at the fund-raiser or persuade others to do so, there's no reason why you couldn't be a perfect candidate for board membership.

In many cases, boards will deem your professional title, your age, or your education to be less important than the ideas, enthusiasm, dedication, and determination you bring to the table. As with any paid or unpaid position you take on, it's up to you to show them why you're valuable. If you haven't done it already, completing the self-assessment in Part I will go a long way toward revealing just what great gifts you have to contribute.

HOW MUCH TIME WILL IT TAKE?

As with everything else we've mentioned in this book, it depends. The amount of time you commit to a board can vary a lot depending on how well established the nonprofit is, how much fund-raising is necessary, how many events the board plans, and whether they are collapsing or expanding programs.

In general, however, board membership can be a long-term commitment (because it takes a while for people to learn what they need to know to be effective), often requiring anywhere from one to three years of service.

The frequency with which local boards meet is set by their bylaws, and can range from once a month to once a quarter to once a year. National boards usually schedule at least one face-to-face meeting per year. And in some instances, meetings can be done by phone. In between meetings, members of some boards spend time on specific tasks, often through a committee geared toward furthering the nonprofit's goals. The size of the organization the board serves affects the range of tasks and responsibilities of its members, which can range from planning and organizing events or networking and asking for donations, to a host of other activities if the organization doesn't have the staff to handle them. Your experience serving on the board of a university or the opera will vastly differ from your experience if you serve on the board of the local park beautification group.

Consider the experience of the board members we introduced at the beginning of this chapter. If we break down their qualifications, responsibilities, and time commitments, it's clear that each one's experience at his or her respective (hypothetical) organization is greatly different from the other.

MARINA

TITLE	ORGANIZATION	FINANCIAL COMMITMENT	TIME COMMITMENT	RESPONSIBILITIES
Board vice president	In Flux: Helps women move from successful careers to their next productive chapter	$2,000/year	One day every two months; informally, about 10 hours/ week	Shape policy, secure investments; head service committee

LEONORA

TITLE	ORGANIZATION	FINANCIAL COMMITMENT	TIME COMMITMENT	RESPONSIBILITIES
Board treasurer	Grandparents from the Heart: Provides opportunities for senior citizens to mentor and participate in the lives of special needs children	$5,000/year	Six meetings a year; annual site visits to hospitals, day cares, public schools, and institutional facilities	Fund-raising, budget development, financial oversight

JAKE

TITLE	ORGANIZATION	FINANCIAL COMMITMENT	TIME COMMITMENT	RESPONSIBILITIES
Board member	Global Hosteling: Promotes hosteling among travelers age eighteen to thirty	None	Eight hours a month, including board meetings	Provide strategic direction, act as community ambassador, fund-raise, add perspective as member of target demographic

ALAN

TITLE	ORGANIZATION	FINANCIAL COMMITMENT	TIME COMMITMENT	RESPONSIBILITIES
Board member	Release the Spirit Ministries: Supports men in their efforts to lead lives according to Christian tenets	Flexible	Monthly meetings	Chair the Community-building Committee, fundraising, strategic planning, event planning

EMMA

TITLE	ORGANIZATION	FINANCIAL COMMITMENT	TIME COMMITMENT	RESPONSIBILITIES
Board member	Fleur de Lys Montessori: Provides Montessori preschool education in a French-speaking environment	None	One board meeting per month; hours per week vary according to what needs to be done	Compile information for newsletter, coordinate volunteer opportunities, schedule school tours

HOW WILL I KNOW WHAT TO DO?

Even if you're already involved in a nonprofit organization, the board can seem like a remote, exotic island on which only the initiated can spread their beach towels. Here's the thing, though—with a few exceptions, no board members know what they're doing when they first join a board. For this reason many boards organize board orientations to familiarize new members with the group's fund-raising responsibilities and bylaws. These events or training sessions also serve as a way of allowing the group to get acquainted and set everyone at ease.

If no formal training program is offered, just listen. Listen to how people communicate at meetings, pay attention to the dynamics within the group, read everything you can about the organization, and most importantly, talk to other board members. They will probably enjoy sharing their wisdom and experience with you. A good board works together as a coherent team—it's in the members' best interest and that of the nonprofit to get you up to speed as quickly as possible.

JOINING THE RIGHT BOARD

Let's say you have come to the conclusion that you have some skills or contacts or experience that will allow you to make an important contribution as a nonprofit board member. Unless you're already actively involved in a nonprofit and want to take on more of a leadership position there, how do you decide which board to serve on?

> One site that matches boards with interested members is BoardnetUSA (www.boardnetusa.com).

Approach your board search the same way you would the search for any job. True, board service is an unpaid volunteer position, yet if you are selected, you will be expected to take the responsibility as seriously as you would in any paid job, especially since you have a legal fiduciary responsibility to the group. That means that you are legally obligated to make decisions—financial, structural, strategic—that are in the best interest of the organization you are serving. This responsibility is one that must be taken seriously; should the group make a decision that results in the organization being forced to close down, and people are owed money, the board could be liable in a lawsuit (many boards offer board insurance for this reason). Make sure the position works for you so that you can make a sustainable commitment. You should be in it for the long haul.

> Researching the board position you want is a lot more fun than looking for a job, precisely because of its unpaid nature. Think about it—this will likely be the first time you have the freedom to do work that you love, that you are good at, and that will garner respect without having to worry about the implications of title or salary. It can be a liberating experience.

There are certain professions—law, finance, real estate, business, and medicine among others—in which it can be a boon to your career to have your name included on the letterhead of a large, well-established nonprofit. If you're in one of these fields, you may be tempted to apply to the nonprofit that has listed the highest number of colleagues from your firm, or that appears most often in the society pages and the news.

But just as it may be a bad idea to apply to a university or job just because that's what your peers are doing, it's inadvisable to join a board for the sake of your professional advancement if it's at the expense of your interests and passion. Imagine how dreadful it would be to go to work every day at a job that held no interest to you (and if this is you, we're delighted you're reading, but you might also want to read a book about how to get your new dream job, pronto!). Although board membership won't take as much time as a full-time job, it still requires a commitment of time, responsibility, and emotional investment. Why waste such precious resources on a cause that doesn't mean anything to you? You'll do more good and get more personal and professional benefits by joining the board of a nonprofit whose cause and mission excites and motivates you.

> Evan Smith, president and editor in chief of *Texas Monthly*, said at a gathering of nonprofits in Austin that he joined the board of a city museum not because he gave a damn about art, but because he gave a damn about Austin and believed it deserved to have a world-class museum. His point was that while your heart doesn't necessarily have to be entirely devoted to the nonprofit's cause, it does have to be devoted to something that dovetails with the best interests of that nonprofit and its mission.

Boards, like organizations, evolve with time. The responsibilities of board members in an emerging organization might be completely different five years down the road. In the early days of establishing the agency, board members might serve not only in an advisory capacity but in a very hands-on way as well—fixing the fax machine, writing the newsletter, maintaining the office space, recruiting and coordinating volunteers, all in addition to attending meetings during which they might discuss whether there is enough money in the budget to hire a part-time employee. As the organization grows, the board may delegate the day-to-day running of the organization to a small staff or even to volunteers while they concentrate on establishing policy and strategic planning for the group's future. Maybe their client base changes and they need more Latinos to represent the community. Their give/get requirements may change, and since there is a limit as to how many board members can join, they may feel required to ramp up the financial contributions of their board. Eventually, if the nonprofit becomes well established and finds itself managing significant funds, members may focus exclusively on setting policy and overseeing the governance of the organization. Their "hands-on" work may evolve into communicating with the organization's executives, managing investments, fund-raising, and recruiting individuals with enough cash or clout to help ensure the group gains recognition in the media and is financially secure.

When considering which board you might like to join, revisit the criteria we listed in the Things to Consider section of Chapter 3, designed to help you choose a nonprofit where you might like to volunteer. The scope, culture, size, and reputation of a nonprofit will of course affect how the board works, who joins it, and how effective it is at accomplishing its goals. For example, is the board purely a fund-raising entity, or is it a working board, in which members get involved in administration and events as well? Large nonprofit boards don't generally need to get involved in day-to-day activities because there is enough infrastructure in place to make sure there is sufficient staff in the office and volunteers in the field to pursue the non-profit's mission. Then again, you may have enough on your plate and not want to participate in the daily activities that make an organization run smoothly, in which case a fund-raising board will be a perfect opportunity to share your guidance and advice. Another question you should consider is whether the board is newly formed, still hammering out procedures and goals, or whether it has been established for years. The answer to this question will determine whether the board will welcome new ideas and any creative solutions you may have to offer, or whether there will already be a pattern of best practice in place that you will be expected to learn and follow. Completing the self-assessment in Chapter 4 will also help you figure out which type of board you would be happiest serving on.

Whatever you do, don't be afraid to visit, especially if you are recruited to join a nonprofit with which you are unfamiliar. Drop in, check out the organization. What does it look and sound like when they're not trying to impress visitors or potential donors? Give them a call—do you like how they talk to you on the phone? Is this an organization with which you will be proud to be associated? Is the location convenient to your work or home? These may seem like basic questions, but many people forget to think about them when caught up in the excitement of imagining themselves at the helm of an organization.

HOW DO I FIND A BOARD OPPORTUNITY?

Often boards will know they have to replace or add a member and will ask around for recommendations from other boards and nonprofits. They may also look within their own organization to see who is a regular, dedicated volunteer. So if you want to be on a board, the best place to start is by serving with that organization. This will give you some valuable experience, confirm your commitment to the group, and possibly get you on the board's radar.

Board service seems to be a club where once you begin, more opportunities are presented. I joined the first board because I wanted to serve GLBTQ youth of color. It was not in my local community, but rather a national organization. I looked online and saw that the members of the board were not people who had greater social status than me, nor did they have my set of skills. I decided to write someone at the organization and let them know that I was interested in their work and would be interested in chatting about joining their board. I spoke with the ED and another member of the board and ultimately completed a board application. Months later I joined their board, where I served for three years.

When I served on a second board, it was with a national organization that sought my participation. They approached me via email, and after several conversations I became convinced that this was worth my time.

Board three came about because I wanted to volunteer locally. When I told the organization what I was interested in doing for them, they looked at my skills and experiences and suggested that I might be a really good addition to their board.

—Russ Finkelstein, board member; Nonprofit Sector Workforce Coalition, City Hall Fellows; Portland, Oregon

Theoretically you could approach a board on your own even without any previous involvement with the nonprofit. Your rate of success will depend a lot on your personality, the kinds of skills you can bring to the table, and the structure of the organization. Should you get as far as an interview, you'll want to impress upon the board members the good reasons why you want to serve as a board member without volunteering first. If you have a very specific skill set they need (or, quite frankly, if you have access to a lot of money), they might vote you in.

A better way to find a spot on a board, however, might be through the online site Boardnet USA (www.boardnetusa.org/public/home.asp). It offers boards the opportunity to connect with individuals interested in board service, and vice versa. Depending on your age, Youth on Board (www.youthonboard

---

GOOD THINGS TO KNOW

QUESTIONS YOU SHOULD ASK THE BOARD BEFORE JOINING

How often do you meet?
How long must I serve?
Am I required to donate a specific amount of money?
What kind of training will I receive?
Will I be required to speak to the media?
Will I be required to fund-raise?
How much will I be involved in the activities of the nonprofit?
How big is the organization?
What's the organization's budget?
Is the organization in good financial health?
Where does the organization get its funding?
Does the board have a long-term plan?

.org) might also be a good resource. It focuses on promoting youth board service, for the most part on the boards of youth-serving organizations.

BOARD POSITIONS

As we've noted, there are many kinds of boards, and their requirements will vary according to their primary function and size. Not every board member has to take on the title and responsibility of an officer; however the following positions are usually established to keep the nonprofit running smoothly:

Chair/President. The chair reports to the board and is ultimately responsible, together with the other members, for any decisions made on behalf of the organization. Like everyone else on the board, his or her job is to preserve and promote the agency's mission and well-being, and it is up to the chair to make sure that all decisions made by the board are to that end. It is the chair's mandate to make sure that all relevant information has been collected and reviewed before any decisions are finalized. For example, if an organization is interested in buying a piece of property on which to build new headquarters, the chair will be in charge of confirming that the board solicits an appropriate number of bids, that they abide by zoning regulations, that they hire a reputable and competitively priced contractor, that the building is made to code, and that all legal issues and financial transactions are handled in an aboveboard and transparent fashion.

While chairs or presidents are allowed to delegate, and should know whom to turn to for objective professional advice when necessary, they are not able to pass on decision-making responsibilities. Such overarching responsibilities necessitate that a Chair have a familiarity with budgets, contracts, bylaws, and, of course, fund-raising. Clearly this is not a position for the faint of heart. But aside from the necessary expertise, it is a great opportunity for a highly organized, detail-oriented individual who is willing to work to secure the organization's best interest at all times. We'd venture to say it is also a position that one can aspire to after serving an appropriate amount of time in other positions within the board.

Secretary. As in any organization, the secretary takes (or approves) minutes at every board meeting to record what issues were brought to the table, what decisions were made, who agreed to take on what tasks, and what points of discussion will need to be brought up at the following meeting. In addition, with nonprofits being asked more and more to make their financial decisions and transactions as transparent as possible, the secretary provides a vital resource for anyone who later wishes to look back on a meeting to confirm that protocol was followed.

Anyone with administrative or legal experience and good writing skills could be an excellent candidate for this position.

Treasurer. The role of the treasurer varies depending on the age and size of an organization and its board. For a new or small nonprofit, it's crucial that someone with solid financial expertise take on this role, particularly if the board chair doesn't have much experience in handling a group's financial matters. A larger or more well-established nonprofit may be able to hire a paid employee or even an entire department to administer and manage the organization's money and support the treasurer's volunteer work on the board.

Just as the secretary keeps records of the proceedings in a meeting, in smaller organizations the treasurer may also be in charge of keeping records of all the organization's financial transactions, including bank deposits and withdrawals, and drafting checks in the name of the agency. The treasurer also develops or presents a budget for the board's approval.

Any one of these positions would be an invaluable opportunity to broaden your leadership experience, stretch your professional skills and natural talents, and make a lasting impact on a nonprofit. But don't knock yourself if you're not interested in taking on one of these more visible roles on the board. Teamwork on boards is essential—you'll find many other ways to make your mark and have an impact.

YOU'RE OFFERED THE POSITION. NOW WHAT?

As with any job, you can negotiate. And of course, as with any job, the board has the right to refuse your requests. But you always have the right to ask for anything that will help make the board service experience a truly great one for you. For example, if you discover that the board requires a financial donation that is too steep, suggest a different sum and offer to do a task that might offset the money that you wouldn't be paying directly from your pocket. Figure out how much you're willing to contribute, whether it's time or money or personal contacts, and ask if that will suit their needs. If it doesn't, there's another board at another nonprofit that will happily take what you've got to give.

IDEALISM IN ACTION

THE BOARD OF DIRECTORS HAS [AN IMPORTANT ROLE] IN SETTING A VISION AND DIRECTION FOR THE ORGANIZATION, AND TO SET AN ENERGIZING TONE FOR STAFF AND OTHER VOLUNTEERS. I GET EXCITED AND IMPASSIONED BEING PART OF THAT TYPE OF ENERGY AND ENGINE. I LEARN SO MUCH FROM BEING AT THE BOARD TABLE. I DO WANT TO NOTE THAT A LOT OF PEOPLE ON BOARDS ARE ALREADY WORKING FULL-TIME JOBS,

MYSELF INCLUDED. BUT WHEN YOU ARE PASSIONATE ABOUT THE ORGANIZATION OR THE ISSUE, YOU FIND THE TIME SOMEHOW TO DO THE BOARD WORK. PART OF THE CHALLENGE OF SERVING ON A BOARD IS TO DISCOVER HOW YOUR OWN PERSONAL HISTORY OR CULTURE OF WORKING INTERACTS WITH OTHERS ON THE BOARD AND THE ORGANIZATION AS A WHOLE. ORGANIZATIONS AND BOARDS ARE CONSTANTLY EVOLVING, AS THEY SHOULD, AND BEING A PART OF THAT EVOLUTION IS IMPORTANT. THE BEST PART [OF SERVING ON A BOARD] IS THE CONNECTING AND RELATIONSHIP BUILDING WITH INSPIRING LEADERS AND BEING EXPOSED TO THEIR ENERGY, THEIR THINKING, AND THEIR DIFFERENT LENSES. THE GENERATIVE DIALOGUE THAT TAKES PLACE AT BOARD MEETINGS IS INSPIRATIONAL.

—Justin Ho, president, board of directors, Volunteer BC and board director
of the HR Council for the Voluntary & Nonprofit Sector;
Vancouver, British Columbia, Canada

Everything You Need to Know About Personal Philanthropy

Like board service, philanthropy is sometimes perceived as reserved for the wealthy and privileged. It's a concept that usually only crosses our radar when we read in the papers about a gala for a local museum or other cultural institution. We look at the accompanying photo spread of prominent members of society in their tuxedoed and sequined splendor and think, "Philanthropy. That's for rich people, not someone like me."

> You'll recall that at Idealist.org we consider everyone who donates money to support a cause or organization to be a philanthropist. We make no distinction between the goodwill of a donor of modest means and that of a wealthier person who can contribute large sums of money.

Alternatively, for many of us, being philanthropic can be a knee-jerk reaction, often triggered by emergencies. We whip out our checkbooks when a news story breaks about a natural disaster, such as Hurricane Ike or the tsunami in Indonesia, when the images of millions of people who have lost everything compel us to do what we can to ease their suffering. More commonly, we'll be walking along or pull up to a red light and someone will ask us if we can spare some change. Whether we give or not will depend entirely upon our mood, how easily we can access our wallet, how long the light lasts, and how trustworthy or suspicious we judge the person asking us for help to be.

Lastly, unless it's a long way off the grid, it's a rare email or physical address that doesn't receive its share of pleas for donations, the number of which seems to quintuple around the holidays. When confronted with these campaigns, you might do one of two things: give on impulse and out of guilt, without thinking too much about the amount, to a couple of randomly chosen charities, or give your standard amount to the charity or charities you have always supported, but feel a twinge of regret that you can't do more. It's also possible that, frustrated by the never-ending stream of appeals, you won't give at all, deleting every email and tossing every unsolicited envelope, unopened, into the trash.

Giving on impulse can feel great. But if you give money and don't feel great about it, or you forget year to year to whom you've given, or you simply wish you could give more, you might consider taking a more proactive approach to donating. For some, all this means is using a little foresight. For example, you might create a savings account into which you can deposit small amounts of money throughout the year, the total of which is earmarked for donations. But many others might benefit from creating a simple donation plan. A donation plan is a financial contribution strategy that will allow you to focus on the specific charities and nonprofits that are most aligned with your values and the causes that you'd like to promote. In addition, you'll maximize how much you can give while staying well within your budget and continuing to lay the groundwork for a healthy financial future, leaving plenty of room for those times when you're compelled to write a check to ease another's suffering (or to load up on Girl Scout cookies).

This chapter will also reveal that philanthropy isn't limited to donating wads of cash. The word "philanthropy" stems from the Greek *phil*, "loving," and *anthropos*, "humanity"—the roots of the word are not tied to money. Read on, and you'll see that there are many, many nonmonetary ways to be generous and show you care about your fellow person (or animal, or forest, as the case may be).

> Volunteers are critical to most organizations, but they don't keep the lights on and pay the salaries of the employees. Even if you can only make a small gift, it keeps you connected to the organization. I think it's a great chance to put your values into action and reflect on the fact that most of us are blessed to have much more than we need, and much more than many other people.
>
> —Caroline Altman Smith, donor, Girls Incorporated, Emerging Practitioners in Philanthropy; Troy, Michigan

CREATING A DONATION PLAN

Two Preliminary Questions

Much as potential volunteers or board members should examine their motives and needs before deciding where they want to contribute their time and/or expertise (see Chapter 1), anyone interested in contributing money to an organization should also give the matter some thought. So the first step in creating a sustainable, successful, and personally rewarding donation plan is to conduct a two-part self-assessment:

1. *What do you need and believe?* You've heard this before. In Part I we encouraged you to think deeply about what matters to you, what you hope to get from your experience with a nonprofit, making sure to consider the organization's structure, culture, and even location. Though a donor won't need to worry about many of the considerations that affect a volunteer, some questions are still relevant when deciding which nonprofit(s) you'd like to support, such as:

   - What issue is most on your mind right now? Why?
   - Where do you perceive the greatest need?
   - What causes, issues, or problems would you find most exciting and emotionally fulfilling to be involved with?
   - What nonprofits, if any, have touched your life or the lives of those around you?
   - Are you interested in having an impact on a local, national, or global level?
   - Would you feel better about supporting a well-established organization or contributing to an emerging nonprofit?

- Does scale matter? If you have $200 to give, would you prefer it go to an organization with a modest budget so you can have greater impact, or would you rather give to a group based on the work they do, regardless of their assets?

> If you're considering donating to a charity, you can check on the financial health of more than five thousand of them at Charity Navigator (www.charitynavigator.org).

2. *What do you value?* Even if the most you are able to donate is $50 to your local health clinic, keep in mind that you are doing more than paying for expenses or supporting a program; you are sending a message about your values. For example, you're making a statement by choosing to give that $50 to the clinic that offers support and prenatal care to pregnant mothers yet no birth control counseling, versus one that offers family planning options. Thinking about what you value, what message about your values you want to send, will ensure that you'll feel great about financially supporting the nonprofit you eventually choose.

By the way, we're not suggesting you trumpet your charitable inclinations to the world, but there is no need to hide them, either. Regardless of where you donate, your act of giving reveals much about your beliefs in the importance of sharing what you have, about the value and purpose of money, and even about the meaning of work. That's a message worth sharing, for who knows how your act of generosity will inspire others.

It is hard to give advice about how to start donating, since each person's situation as a donor is different. First one must feel that there are resources to spare. Once it is clear that there is security at home, there are many ways to consider what amount to give. Then I guess I would just say, "Start!" You can learn as you go. Make gifts that feel important to you and learn as much as you can about which nonprofits are doing the job they promise to do.

—Lucy Stroock, donor, Population Media Center, Peace Action, Cambridge Early Childhood Programs, South Indian Girl Child Project, ACCION; Cambridge, Massachusetts

SO MANY WAYS TO GIVE

Once you lay the philosophical groundwork of your donation plan—what you need and what you value—it's time to review the many, many ways in which you can make a lasting impression on a nonprofit through a donation, whatever your assets.

Now, you may be thinking, "Assets? What assets? I wish I had assets." OK, so not all of us have savings to spare, or investments and real estate. But you might have more than you realize. For example, do you have a family member who sends you a payout from a mature CD every year? Do you ever get gift cards for your birthday or around the holidays? Do you have life insurance? Do you know that eventually you will inherit a piece of property or maybe a coin collection? We're going to show you how any of these resources can be transformed into a donation that can help the organization you like best. Whether you earned it, saved it, or inherited it, the money you donate gives you an opportunity to do great good. That's something to be excited about.

We'll start with the most popular and commonly available options for giving, and then introduce more sophisticated, resource-dependent opportunities. This is just an overview to familiarize you with the available options, and is by no means complete. (It would take an entire book filled with technical financial jargon to elaborate on all the complexities inherent in some of these possible gifts.) Idealists who are able to consider some of the options beyond simple cash donations should get the advice of an experienced financial planner who can make sure their generosity will be of maximum value to their chosen nonprofit(s) while also allowing them to take advantage of any fringe benefits attached to that particular donation strategy.

We should also note that although we want you to be aware of all the giving options available, the reality is that the fastest way to make a difference is to keep things simple. So as you read about the various personal philanthropy opportunities out there, keep two things in mind:

1. Chances are good that you already know an organization that needs your support—a homeless shelter, community theater, day care center, senior drop-in program.

2. Although many donor options will give you the choice of how and when you want your money to be spent or your assets allocated, the people running these nonprofits are the best judges of where a donation can be most effectively used. It's OK to trust these leaders to make wise financial decisions. If you're extremely concerned about knowing how money is spent at a nonprofit, you might consider becoming a leader yourself by volunteering or serving on the board. There's no better way to get to know an organization inside and out.

Donating Cash

Nonprofits love cash donations. Organizations are under constant pressure to minimize their expenses yet maximize their services. Boards review and adjust budgets, clients request additional help, the cost of basic necessities and office supplies rise every year. So every nonprofit is grateful for whatever funds it receives, whether it's $10, $100, or $100,000, and you can feel good knowing you are keeping them afloat. Cash is always good.

ADVANTAGES
- Simplicity
- Practicality
- You may receive an immediate tax deduction

- The organization has instant access to dollars that can be used for whatever needs are most pressing at the time of your donation

Some religions encourage their followers to donate specific percentages of their income. Tithing—offering one-tenth of one's gross income to church, charity, or a combination of both—has become a popular standard of giving in many Christian denominations. One of the Five Pillars of Islam—the five obligations of every Muslim—is *Zakat*, or donating 2.5 percent of one's personal value to the poor. Some Jews practice *tzedakah*, the obligation to give 10 percent of one's income to charity. Most religions encourage some kind of stewardship or charitable giving, even if they don't specify how much.

How Much Should I Give? That's entirely up to you. The amount you decide to give will depend on your individual financial circumstances as well as your philosophical, spiritual, and practical attitudes toward money.

One longtime donor we spoke with suggested that individuals who are looking for a donation guideline might keep in mind that the average American gives 2 percent of his or her pretax income to charity. Thus, if you were inclined to use that statistic as your benchmark, you could calculate 2 percent of your salary as your philanthropic budget for the year, much as you would any other household expense. Even if you can't jump in at the 2 percent level, you could start out with 1 percent, with the goal of eventually increasing to 2 percent.

Or you can decide upon a fixed amount that you are

willing to donate, and go from there. Regardless, be sure to consider not just your income but also your assets when establishing a reasonable target. In figuring the amount of your charitable giving, there is no better or worse, no right or wrong.

There are excellent resources where you can go to get more information, even formulas, for evaluating your assets. You might start with:

Bolder Giving: www.boldergiving.org. Provides inspirational stories, coaching, resources, and tools, including quizzes, hotlines, and workshops.

Resource Generation: www.resourcegeneration.org. Click on "Resources" for a comprehensive list of websites, publications, and organizations that can help you.

Inspired Philanthropy: Your Step-By-Step Guide To Creating a Giving Plan, 2nd Edition, by Tracy Gary and Melissa Kohner. San Francisco: Jossey-Bass, 2002.

> **The next time you're thinking of selling something online, remember that you can donate a percentage of any sale on eBay through Mission-Fish (www.missionfish.org).**

Alternatives to Giving Cash

There are many less familiar yet perfectly acceptable ways to make an immediate impact on a nonprofit's bottom line. Have you ever received a gift card to a store that you don't frequent very often? Rather than let it languish in your desk until it expires, how about donating it to a nonprofit? Most organizations run events and would be grateful for supplies from any store. In particular, nonprofits can use gift cards to big box stores such as Wal-Mart, Costco, Sam's, Home Depot, Lowe's, or OfficeMax. Gift cards to Target or department stores can also be extremely helpful, especially to any organization that serves the homeless, battered women, or families in need. An animal shelter could use a card to PETCO. A school could use one to Teacher Heaven. Donating a gift card is also an excellent way to specify how you want your money spent. So if your intent is to help ease the transportation costs for an organization that helps the elderly get to and from doctor visits, a gas card is an excellent choice.

What about airline mileage? Most organizations have to send their staff to meetings that often take place in other parts of the country. Many airlines are starting to put limits on how long a person can hold on to accumulated miles. If you're reasonably sure you're not going to be able to use all of your mileage before it expires, or if you have accumulated a lot of miles through business travel, consider donating them to an organization like the Make-A-Wish Foundation, or Doctors Without Borders, or to Operation Hero Miles, which allows servicemen and -women serving in Iraq or Afghanistan to fly home on leave for free, or family members of wounded soldiers to travel to see their loved ones at the military hospital where they are recuperating.

> There are other items one can donate, such as equipment, vehicles, or other gifts of "related use," which we'll discuss a little later, as they may require slightly more complicated arrangements.

Even More Alternatives to Giving Cash

You've probably already heard of Goodwill and the Salvation Army, which are terrific organizations that accept a wide variety of items for donations (just call and ask if you're not sure what you've got in your basement is something they'll take) and you might be familiar with a few local institutions that sponsor food drives in your area. But did you know there are nonprofits where you can donate yarn? Musical instruments? Batteries? The list of items that can be donated to a nonprofit is a long one, and some might surprise you.

DONATION	NONPROFIT	WEB ADDRESS
Art supplies	Artists Helping Children	www.artistshelpingchildren.org
Artwork	Art for Healing	www.artforhealing.org
Baby clothes	Newborns in Need	www.newbornsinneed.org
Batteries	Rechargeable Battery Recycling Corporation	www.rbrc.org
Bicycles	Pedals for Progress	www.p4p.org
Books	American Library Association Book Donation Programs www.ala.org/ala/alalibrary/libraryfactsheet/alalibraryfactsheet12.cfm	

(continued)

DONATION	NONPROFIT	WEB ADDRESS
Breast milk	National Milk Bank	www.nationalmilkbank.org
Cell phones	Wireless Foundation	www.donateaphone.com
Coats	One Warm Coat	www.onewarmcoat.org
Dresses	Dress for Success	www.dressforsuccess.org
Eyeglasses	Unite for Sight	www.uniteforsight.org
Food	America's Second Harvest	www.secondharvest.org
Footballs	Sports Gift Inc.	www.sportsgift.org
Galoshes	Goodwill Industries	www.goodwill.org
Hair	Locks of Love	www.locksoflove.org
Hearing aids	So the World May Hear	www.sotheworldmayhear.org
Inkjet and laser cartridges	Share the Technology	www.sharetechnology.org
Jigsaw puzzles	nursing homes	www.nursinghomedirectory.org
Knitting	Wool Works	www.woolworks.org/charity.html
Laptops	One Laptop Per Child	www.laptopgiving.org
Movies	Ronald McDonald House	www.rmhc.com
Notebooks	I Love Schools	www.iloveschools.com
Orthotics	Orthotic and Prosthetic Assistance Fund	www.opfund.org
Pajamas	Pajama Project	www.pajamaprogram.org
Prom dresses	Princess Project	www.princessproject.org
Quilts	Project Linus	www.projectlinus.org

DONATION	NONPROFIT	WEB ADDRESS
Rawhide dog chews	Your local pet rescues	www.petfinder.com
Suits	Working Wardrobes	www.workingwardrobes.org
Tools	Tool Lending Libraries	Google search in your state
Toys	Kids in Distressed Situations	www.kidsdonations.org
Unused frequent-flier miles	Mile Donor	www.miledonor.com
Wheelchairs	Wheelchair Foundation	www.wheelchairfoundation.org
Xylophones	Charity Music	www.charitymusic.org
Yarn	Warm Woolies	www.warmwoolies.org
Zither	Mr. Holland's Opus Foundation	www.mhopus.org

Keep this list in mind the next time you're doing your spring cleaning! And if you're ever staring at something—a motorcycle, office furniture, old costumes—and wondering whether there's a charity out there that would accept it, try doing a search through Google.

Fund-Raising

Another way to engage in philanthropy if you don't have a lot of money of your own is to get other people to donate through fund-raising. People with entrepreneurial spirit often go this route in response to a natural disaster or other catastrophic event, but it can be done even just to ensure that your local Little League team has uniforms for the season.

Host a house party. As a price of admission ask for two cans of nonperishable food or for guests to be willing to listen to a five-minute talk about a cause or nonprofit (and then be sure to pass the hat!). Another easy way to host a fund-raiser is through a Fund-Raiser in a Box, which you'll find on the websites of some organizations. It generally gives you a one-stop-shopping option for all your fund-raising materials. For example, the Wounded Warrior Project will send you flyers, lapel pins, an informational DVD, and a folder with FAQs and best practices to make your fund-raiser a success.

There are various kinds of fund-raising. For more information, try the following websites:

Fund-Raising for Groups:
www.amnestyusa.org/run-your-group/how-to-raise-funds-the-basics/page.do?id=1031050&n1=4&n2=63&n3=131

Fund-Raising for Kids:
www.justgive.org/html/kidscorner/fund-raise.html

Fund-Raising to Raise Money for a Trip:
www.globalcrossroad.com/humanitariantrips/how-to-raise-fund.php

Fund-raising is an admirable impulse but not quite as simple as collecting money from people and then signing over a single check. We strongly advise that people link their efforts to an established charity that either has fund-raising staff or has proven experience with successful fund-raising. (Many nonprofits will welcome volunteers who are willing to organize fund-raisers or work on events already in progress.) Otherwise it will be up to you to ascertain that the charity you want to fund-raise for is itself in compliance with charitable giving laws, something that is extremely difficult to confirm. A few tips to help you avoid some of the more complicated legal issues that can arise when you try to fund-raise on your own:

1. Target a particular organization. Don't just start collecting money for a general cause with the recipient of the money to be determined after the fact.

2. Many organizations have policies about fund-raising in their name because of the risk of frauds using their organization as a front to collect money and keep it for themselves. In fact, in some states it is illegal to fund-raise in a charity's name without a signed agreement. Before launching your fund-raiser, contact the nonprofit and inform them of your plan. Make sure that your message and goals are aligned with the cause you are trying to help.

3. Many states or counties have charitable solicitation laws in place to regulate fund-raising. The rules are summarized at www.multistatefiling.org. (This website was created to help big organizations asking for donations in multiple states, but the state-by-state index of regulations will give you a sense of whether you will need to talk with your local charity oversight officials before starting your campaign.)

4. Be sure not to mix up the funds you raise in your campaign with your own money. Open a separate bank account that will be used only for the campaign so that if the IRS or your local tax department asks to see records, you can prove that the funds were kept separate and should not be considered taxable earned income.

5. Tax deductions depend on the givers' tax situation and only apply to certain gifts and nonprofits, so don't promise donors that their contribution will be tax deductible until you have all the information.

6. Approach local institutions to see if they are willing to help. Many banks and churches will set up accounts to receive donations intended to defray the costs of a victim's hospital bills, to rebuild after a disaster, or scholarship/memorial funds in the event of a death.

- You have an immediate impact on the organization without dipping into your cash flow
- You may feel more secure in how your charitable donation will be used

> **Some hotel and credit card loyalty programs also allow you to donate reward points to charity.**

Planned Giving

Your donation plan doesn't have to be a one-way street. Donating cash or cash alternatives provides immediate help to organizations and gives you a terrific emotional return on investment, but you can benefit a charity and benefit yourself at the same time. For those individuals who have access to family money, who own property or business, or who have simply been around long enough to accumulate a few financial assets, "planned giving" is the formal term used to describe the think-ahead strategy of donating money or assets to a nonprofit in such a way as to also protect or even improve your financial future. With planned giving, you can take advantage of tax breaks and other policies in place that reward and encourage generosity like yours, including the ability to pass assets to your family after your death at a reduced tax cost. In some cases it can even provide you with a steady stream of income.

There are eight strategies available to you through planned giving channels. Clearly not everyone will be eligible to use every strategy—many are designed for people with very specific assets, such as real estate or ownership of a company. Regardless, in every case you will require some assistance with a financial planner or lawyer. (We'd love to help you ourselves, but since we're not financial experts the best we can do is tell you that these options exist.) These experts in the field are there to help you make sound financial decisions and make sure that it is in your best interest to make a donation. Even if you are financially savvy, go to the nonprofit's website and/or speak to the organization's planned giving coordinator for information and guidance on how to get started. Taking these preliminary steps may make the process sound complicated or expensive, but the small upfront investment of time and money is worth it in the end.

Eight Planned Donor Strategies

1. Give Stocks and Bonds. Owning stocks and bonds can be a great way to build wealth, but it comes with a downside: when you sell, you're hit with a capital gains tax on the money you earned over time. By donating gifts of appreciated securities (the technical term for stocks and bonds) to a nonprofit, you can avoid that tax and enjoy knowing your money has gone to a cause that matters to you.

> Since the value of most stocks varies all the time, for tax purposes the final value of your donation is calculated by averaging the high and low prices of the stock or bond on the day the transfer is made.

- Allows you to make a larger gift to the nonprofit than might otherwise be possible, because you avoid paying capital gains tax
- You can make a significant donation without making a dent in your liquidity (the money you already have available to live on and enjoy)
- You receive an immediate charitable tax deduction

2. Name a Nonprofit in Your Will. There are many people who would love to make a financial donation to an organization but just don't feel comfortable parting with money they may need in the future. Such prudence is perfectly understandable. So how about donating the money when you're sure you won't need it anymore? By including a bequest to a nonprofit alongside other beneficiaries in your will, your money is at your disposal during your lifetime, you don't limit any potential interest or earnings in your portfolio, and you ensure that the common good is provided for in addition to your beneficiaries. Anything can be bequeathed—cash, securities, real estate, whatever you choose.

ADVANTAGES
- Your money is always available to you during your lifetime
- You can change your bequest at any time
- You have the satisfaction of knowing that you are leaving behind a lasting legacy

- A charitable bequest may reduce any federal or state inheritance or estate taxes

3. Give Retirement Assets. Another way to provide for a nonprofit or other organization after your death while retaining your assets during your lifetime is to donate your IRA, 401(k), or other retirement plan. Just name a charity (or charities) as your beneficiary, or as a contingent beneficiary after family members or other individuals, and when you die it will receive any residual left over.

ADVANTAGES
- You continue to make withdrawals for as long as you need them
- You pay neither income nor estate taxes on the residual once you die
- It's risk free—if you change your mind or your circumstances change, you can easily change the beneficiary named on your retirement plan documents

4. Give Life Insurance. As we get older, we often no longer need as much life insurance as we once did. Often we buy life insurance policies for spouses who pass away before us, or children who then become financially independent. In any of these cases, the life insurance that you or your loved one no longer need could make an excellent financial contribution to a nonprofit that doesn't cost you one additional penny, and in fact may even save you money.

- It won't affect your cash flow, since in most cases it's already paid for
- It can potentially save you money in averted taxes

5. Give to a Pooled Income Fund. A pooled income fund benefits you now and the nonprofit later. It bears a strong similarity to a mutual fund. Your donation of securities or cash is combined with that of other donors and the nonprofit invests the money. The nonprofit keeps the principal while you and your fellow donors each receive a payout, which continues through your lifetime. You can even continue the payments to a beneficiary after your death. In this way you guarantee yourself or your heirs income while still claiming a charitable deduction. Once the last beneficiary of your investment dies, the nonprofit can use the principal to pay for services or expenses, or for the purpose you designate.

ADVANTAGES
- You receive lifetime income
- You receive a charitable tax deduction on a portion of your donation
- You avoid paying capital gains tax on any appreciated assets

6. Give Real Estate. Maybe you inherited a house from Great Aunt Vera, or own a vacation home that you aren't using enough anymore to justify the maintenance expense, or maybe you're ready to sell a piece of land or a commercial property.

Even in soft real estate markets, more and more nonprofits will be willing to accept a donation of property while providing you with significant tax savings, and even income. Other than simply transferring the deed of the property to the nonprofit's name, there are a few ways you can structure your real estate donation:

1. *Retained life estate.* If you want to donate your property to a nonprofit but still need to live in it or use it, you can set up a retained life estate, which allows you to deed the residence to the nonprofit while reserving the right to use it during your lifetime. You have continued access to your property, yet you can receive an immediate income tax deduction and a federal estate tax deduction.

2. *Charitable remainder unitrust.* This flexible plan is another way to make a donation while still earning income from your investments (it's not exclusive to real estate transactions). It works like this: You transfer your property into a trust. The trust then pays you annually a fixed percentage of the value of the principal, which hopefully increases every year and thus gradually increases your income. (If it decreases, then naturally your income will decrease as well.) What's in it for the nonprofit? Any amount of appreciation above that fixed percentage reverts to it to reinvest in the principal, allowing it to grow its assets. Once you or your last beneficiary dies, the nonprofit is then allowed to withdraw the principal.

One type of charitable remainder trust is a flip unitrust, in which you receive no payments until a certain date or event, such as your retirement. It then reverts, or flips, to a standard unitrust and pays you the fixed percentage of the value of the principal. It's an excellent supplemental retirement fund that allows for your money to grow tax free until the date of the flip.

3. *Charitable lead trust.* This plan works the same as a charitable remainder trust, except the recipients of the fixed percentage and the principal are reversed. Therefore, the nonprofit(s) of your choice receive an income stream throughout your lifetime, but after your death it's your beneficiaries who receive the principal. The tax benefits and savings are the same as they would be for a charitable remainder trust.

4. *Charitable annuity trust.* Providing the same charitable and capital gains tax benefits, a charitable annuity trust works in much the same way as the lead trust, except it offers you a fixed annual income instead of one that fluctuates according to the market. With an annuity trust, you will always receive 5 percent of the initial fair market value of your original gift, regardless of whether the principal increases or decreases in value.

ADVANTAGES

- You make a significant donation to a nonprofit while still retaining a lifetime of income for you and/or your heirs

- You receive an immediate charitable tax deduction
- If you have held the property for over a year (which is considered long-term), you don't have to pay taxes on any appreciated value of the property, so you don't get penalized for making a smart investment.

7. Give Your Valuables. *Antiques Roadshow* is coming to your city, and you've always been curious to learn more about that old portrait you inherited from Aunt Vera that's been gathering dust in the attic. On a lark, you take it to the convention center. The appraiser takes one look at your portrait and lights up. Turns out you've been harboring the last in a series by a minor but well-respected eighteenth-century Flemish portraitist. That dusty old picture is worth a lot more than you thought!

Whether you substitute a tea set, a stamp collection, jewelry, or any other possession of value in this example, the end result is the same—once the shock wears off, you'll need to decide what to do with it. The two obvious choices are to hang on to your new treasure or sell it for cash. The third, perhaps less obvious choice is to donate it to charity. The organization then has the option of keeping it, perhaps even displaying it, and allowing it to appreciate further in value, or selling the portrait and using the profits to fund its work.

Not all gifts of this sort need to fall into the luxury goods category. If you donate a van to an animal shelter, which they can use to transport animals, you are entitled to a charitable deduction for the full resale value of the van. Your tax deduction will vary depending on whether your gift falls into what the IRS deems "related use," so not all charities will be appropriate recipients for these kinds of donations.

> **Regardless of what *Antiques Roadshow* or anyone else says your gift is worth, you will need to get an official and independent appraisal of your collection, artwork, or any other personal property you wish to donate.**

ADVANTAGES

- You're giving away something that's never been tallied in your assets, so you'll never miss it when calculating your financial net worth
- If donating a "related use" gift of transportation, supplies, or equipment, you're making a practical, immediately beneficial contribution to the nonprofit's ability to perform its mission
- Assuming your gift fits the description of "related use," you get an immediate income tax deduction and pay no capital gains tax

8. *Give Business Interests.* If you own shares of closely held stock in a corporation, you can donate shares to a nonprofit without getting saddled with the tax penalty you would normally pay if you tried to redeem your stock. Instead, you get an income tax deduction for the value of the shares, while the nonprofit can turn the shares in to the company for redemption. Keep in mind that by donating the shares you are essentially allowing the nonprofit part ownership of the company, and some nonprofits may be unwilling to assume the responsibility such ownership entails. Again, your financial planner or a planned giving coordinator can help you set this up.

ADVANTAGES
- Immediate charitable income tax deduction for the value of the shares
- As usual, you avoid paying capital gains tax

> Closely held stock doesn't trade publicly, so you will need to get the fair market value of the stock appraised in order to determine your charitable deduction.

PUTTING IT TOGETHER

You've established your beliefs, your needs, your values, and the assets you have available. Now you need a tool to help you articulate this information and organize it. That tool is a donation plan. A well laid out donation plan allows you to study your self-assessment, the details of your income and assets, and the answers to a list of key questions to help you pinpoint the ideal recipient for your financial or in-kind contributions.

Let's say that your preliminary assessment led you to the following conclusions:

I BELIEVE
that we must reduce the human footprint on
the environment.

■

I VALUE
the environmental, physical, and community benefits
of public transportation.

■

I NEED
to see the results of my donation and the
organization's efforts.

■

I HAVE
$10,000 in savings, a growing 401(k), a neglected Roth IRA.

■

I CAN COMFORTABLY DONATE
$200 a year.

Now let's consider some additional questions. Keeping in mind your beliefs, values, and needs, what would you be most excited to do, regardless of your financial circumstances?

I WOULD BE EXCITED TO
help my city adopt and embrace public transportation.

Now you can start researching those organizations that you can enthusiastically endorse and support. Questions to ask yourself while you do this are:

1. What organizations do I already know about that do good work?
2. Do I want to spend my money in my local community or internationally?
3. Do I want to put all my money into one agency or spread it out among several?
4. Do I want to allocate the money toward general operational support or a specific program?

As you narrow down your choices, be sure you can answer these particular questions:

1. Are you confident that your money will be spent wisely?
2. Would you be proud for people to know about your affiliation with this organization (even if you never plan to advertise your involvement)?
3. Do you agree with their vision and mission?
4. Do you approve of their strategies for solving the problem or addressing the issue around which they are built?
5. Are you comfortable with the way they present themselves to the media?
6. Are you satisfied with their rate of success?

Most nonprofits are happy to offer information about themselves, and it's perfectly acceptable to request information whether or not you make a financial gift. In addition, the Better Business Bureau's Wise Giving Alliance provides the public with a way to check whether a charity is upholding certain standards (such as the BBB's twenty standards for charity accountability) and information on tax status, governance, fund-raising, and programs. You can also order a free *Wise Giving Guide*. The BBB does not evaluate the worthiness of a charity, and just because a charity is not listed or has not been evaluated doesn't mean you should discount the charity. But at the very least, the site, www.us.bbb.org, is useful for the list of thousands of charities and their corresponding contact information.

Ultimately, your donation plan could look like this:

I BELIEVE
that we must reduce the human footprint on the environment.

■

I VALUE
the environmental, physical, and community benefits of public transportation.

■

I NEED
to see the results of my donation and the organization's efforts.

■

I HAVE
$10,000 in savings, a growing 401(k), a neglected Roth IRA.

■

I CAN COMFORTABLY DONATE
$200 a year.

■

I WOULD BE EXCITED TO
help my city adopt and embrace public transportation.

■

I WILL DONATE
$100 to Liveable City and $100 to Austin CarShare.

Another person's plan might look like this:

I BELIEVE
that tolerance and equality are fundamental values.

■

I VALUE
the message of peace and nonviolence taught by
the church.

■

I NEED
to know that my wealth will help others beyond
my family.

■

I HAVE

the car Mom can't drive anymore, the life insurance plan
I was going to cancel now that Jimmy is on his own and
has a job, a little stock that I can spare.

■

I WOULD BE EXCITED TO

see more resources and information made available to
help children avoid violence.

■

I WILL DONATE

the car and the stock to the Southern Law and
Poverty Center.

Here's the thing about donating money to groups and causes you believe in: it's supposed to feel good. Guilt shouldn't play any part in your decision to give or not to give. And once you do give, you shouldn't feel that you're not doing enough. By creating a donation plan, we avoid the haphazardness and confusion that can plague us when we consider making a philanthropic contribution, leaving nothing but elevated spirits and a sense of accomplishment and pride.

WAIT, DIDN'T WE FORGET SOMETHING?

You may have noticed that in our rundown of all the ways we can make financial contributions to an organization, we neglected to discuss any workplace giving options. We spend a heck of a lot of our time at work; surely we could harness more of the resources we have available to us there to serve the greater good beyond the office walls? As a matter of fact, we can. The next part of the book will explore the unprecedented and exciting ways in which our work environment is changing so as to make such progress possible.

IDEALISM IN ACTION

DONATING FEELS GREAT! BUT I DON'T GIVE TO FEEL GOOD. I GIVE FOR THE RESULTS. IT IS THE RESULTS THAT MATTER. I HAVE MORE MONEY THAN TIME AT THIS STAGE OF MY LIFE. I HAVE VOLUNTEERED IN THE PAST, WHEN I HAD MORE TIME THAN MONEY.

OF ALL THE THINGS I HAVE DONE IN MY LIFE, I VIEW GIVING AS AMONG MY GREATEST ACCOMPLISHMENTS, SECOND ONLY TO RAISING CHILDREN AND HAVING A FAMILY. I FEEL MY GIVING IS SOMETHING THAT CAN'T BE TAKEN AWAY FROM ME. MY FORTUNES MAY CHANGE. WHO CAN PREDICT THE FUTURE? I MIGHT LOSE MY JOB. MY MARRIAGE MIGHT FALL APART. I COULD BECOME ILL OR DISABLED. SURPRISES HAPPEN. IN ALL THE VICISSITUDES OF LIFE, AN ACT OF GENEROSITY ENDURES. OPPORTUNITIES FOR SUCCESS AND ACHIEVEMENT ARE NOT JUST FOR THE RICH. THE ENDURING VALUE OF GENEROSITY APPLIES TO SMALL GIFTS AS WELL AS LARGE. HAVING A LOT OF MONEY IS IRRELEVANT. GIVING IS OPEN TO ALL.

—Cliff Landesman, donor and volunteer; Brooklyn, New York

PART III

Idealism at Work

8

Everything You Need to Know About Changing the World Through Your Workplace

Maintaining a healthy work/life balance is a challenge for many idealists, even when we love our work. When you're getting up at the crack of dawn to get ready for a long commute, then scrambling to get your job done while juggling meetings, emails, clients, and your supervisors' demands, before making the long commute back, it can be hard to fit in other things you enjoy doing, like exercise, hobbies, seeing the latest movie, and yes, do-gooding. More and more time spent at the workplace means less personal time to use for volunteering, board service, or philanthropy.

Luckily, more and more companies are recognizing the morale-boosting effects, not to mention the public relations value, of setting up opportunities for employees to volunteer and donate to various organizations. Even if you don't work for a big company, your employer may contribute to your community more than you realize, and we'll point out some of the ways you can make the most of those contributions by getting involved. If you find that your workplace in fact doesn't participate in any charitable or philanthropic activities, this chapter will offer a number of ways in which you can help get them started, even if you're not the owner or an executive.

> Many companies can and should be lauded for their charitable donations, their employee volunteer programs, and their efforts to reduce their impact on the environment. Then there are companies that practice corporate social responsibility (CSR), in which concern for consumers, the community, and/or the environment helps shape their business strategy and their products or services. We'll examine CSR at length in the next chapter.

HOW COMPANIES CONTRIBUTE

The Fortune 500 firms get a lot of press for their charitable and philanthropic efforts throughout the world, and rightfully so. But small- and medium-size businesses—the ones many of us work for—contribute a tremendous amount to their local and statewide communities.

Without the generosity of American businesses, in fact, most nonprofit organizations simply wouldn't look the same. Some of the ways in which companies engage with local or regional nonprofits are:

Sponsorship

Often when you go past a ball field, you'll see a group of kids wearing matching uniforms with, say, Pino's Pizzeria emblazoned on the back. The ball team needs uniforms, the pizzeria needs name recognition, together they provide a mutual benefit—the kids get the uniforms, the pizzeria gets some advertising. You might also notice that local businesses often sponsor citywide events, such as parades and festivals, or contribute food, T-shirts, or supplies to neighborhood cleanups. Again, the businesses' participation makes a win-win possible for everyone involved—the city boosts civic pride, the community comes together, and local business profits from the marketing, advertising, and goodwill stemming from the event. In addition, there's media sponsorship, where radio, TV, or newspapers will promote an event in exchange for mentions in press releases or space on banners.

Corporate Volunteerism

Corporate volunteer programs have become increasingly popular in the American workplace, especially since the benefits of volunteerism to the company, in addition to the nonprofit or the employee, are now well documented. There are three benefits that are universally cited:

1. More loyal, more productive employees
2. A positive public image

3. Improved management, leadership, public relations, and marketing opportunities for the business

In addition, many companies have learned that employees who are given the chance to participate in skilled volunteering actually enhance their value to the business because they are able to develop leadership techniques and practice their skills in ways they might not be able to at the office.

Corporate volunteer programs can take many different forms:

1. Employees independently volunteer and seek individual support from their employer.
2. The company allots each employee a select number of paid hours to be spent volunteering at the employee's nonprofit of choice.
3. The company chooses a select number of nonprofits to support and announces volunteer opportunities to employees.
4. The company establishes a formal volunteer program and coordinates volunteer opportunities with a select number of nonprofits.
5. The company decides to support one particular organization and encourages employees to contribute their time and skills to that nonprofit, promoting and acknowledging their efforts through the company newsletter or website.
6. The company offers pro bono services to a variety of nonprofit organizations.

Corporate Philanthropy

Corporate America donates billions of dollars to charitable causes and organizations every year. Many of these philanthropic programs are more complicated variations of some of the donor options we discussed in Chapter 7. Just about every company has money available for charity. So why not try to reserve some of your employer's funds for your favorite organization? Whenever you are considering making a philanthropic donation, look into whether your workplace has any of the following programs in place that can help maximize your giving capacity.

Company Match. A simple way to double your donation to a nonprofit is by taking advantage of your workplace's company match program. Once you have determined where you want to make a financial contribution, check with your Human Resources Department or company website for a list of nonprofits the company supports. If yours is one of them, simply fill out the relevant paperwork and send it in to the appropriate party. If your nonprofit isn't among the company's selection, and especially if you are donating in response to a natural disaster or other unique circumstance, find out who is in charge of deciding which organizations the company will match and petition for the one you wish to support. (Many companies will provide matches to any nonprofit in the community, but some give you the option of donating only to a predetermined list of organizations.)

Federated Funds (also known as workplace giving programs). Many businesses offer their employees the option of donating a portion of their paycheck to a federated fund, which then distributes the money to a select group of local nonprofits. You can choose the charity to which you want your donation to go, and then that amount, whether $2, $4, or $100, is automatically deducted from every paycheck. Federated funds are beneficial in many ways: you get a tax deduction, your employer gets recognition for doing good for the local community, and the nonprofit only has to process paperwork for one lump donation. United Way is one of the oldest and most well-recognized federated funds, but there are also other funds that target specific issues affecting the environment, health, arts and culture, or racial minorities. If you weren't informed at the time you joined your company, ask your HR department whether federated funds are available to you. If not, find out whether anyone has ever looked into establishing such a program and make it clear that you'd like to participate should the opportunity arise. If enough people seem interested in the idea, it's possible that HR will take steps toward establishing the program.

You might also investigate a socially responsible fund and ask if your business would consider adding it to their investment choices. These are funds that generally avoid investing in companies that aren't environmentally responsible, produce nuclear technology, promote gambling, or sell tobacco or alcohol products. One site devoted to providing the public with information about socially responsible investment funds is Social Investment Forum (www.socialinvest.org).

Money for Time. If you already volunteer or are about to begin, see if your company has or might consider what Gap calls a money for time program. When Gap employees volunteer fifteen hours for an organization, the company donates $150 to that organization. Microsoft matches employees' volunteer time with a $17 donation for each volunteer hour, up to $12,000 per year. Naturally not all companies can contribute at this financial level, but in the nonprofit world, everything helps. Your time plus your company's financial contribution makes for a valuable boost to helping that nonprofit fulfill its mission.

In-Kind Donations. Many businesses make financial contributions to nonprofits, but they also often donate goods, services, or products—also known as in-kind donations—that can benefit the organization or those it serves. Though there is no requirement that the donation be directly linked to what the company manufactures or sells, that is often how a company feels it can make the most mutually beneficial contribution. Thus a book publisher might donate books to a children's library; a paper manufacturer might donate printer paper for an organization's headquarters; tech companies often provide computer equipment or technical services. Other in-kind donations might include toys, tools, clothing, educational materials, sports equipment, furniture, arts and crafts supplies, and home improvement or construction materials. The concept can also encompass some of the philanthropic contributions we discussed in Chapter 7, such as land or art.

There are plenty of other ways you or the company you work for can donate resources to organizations that don't involve making financial contributions yet have tremendous monetary value. You could suggest or implement any of these ideas:

- Make your conference rooms available for a nonprofit's meetings
- Set up mentoring groups to help improve nonprofit employees' business strategies or technical knowledge
- Allow volunteers to post flyers in common areas or on their office doors

- If your office undergoes a renovation or otherwise replaces furniture, fixtures, or computers, arrange to donate the castoffs
- Find out how to earmark leftover food and beverages from company parties for a local shelter or food bank

In most cases, to implement a program, you should simply call the organization you wish to help and ask them how they want you to proceed, then talk to your HR director (or whoever is high enough up the business ladder to make these decisions) about how you can put your plan into action. For additional inspiration, read Debra Meyerson's *Tempered Radicals: How People Use Difference to Inspire Change at Work.* (You can find an excerpt at http://hbswk.hbs.edu/archive/2538.html.)

> Of course you'll have the best intentions when you initiate a relationship with a nonprofit, but in this case, try to forget the Golden Rule—do unto others as you would have done unto you. Ask, rather, what they would have done unto them; it might be completely different from what you would want for yourself or your company. Never assume you know what the nonprofit needs.

If you're a business owner or a top executive, you could also:

- Offer to use your in-house design team or printing facilities for a group's brochures, invitations, or other materials

- Place a logo and a Web address (URL) for the organization on your next advertisement or on your website
- Include a link, plug, or article about a charity in your next mailing to your customers

WHAT YOU CAN DO

So just how are you supposed to start these programs in your own workplace? For entrepreneurs or business owners, the volunteer or philanthropic opportunity that will work best for you is the one that results in a mutually beneficial relationship between your company and a nonprofit organization. There are resources available to offer you guidance as you determine what programs might fit the bill. Two are particularly comprehensive and useful:

GreenBiz.com offers a free twelve-page pamphlet called "Greening Your Business: A Primer for Smaller Companies," which lists all the ways you can reduce waste, improve energy and water efficiency, control your use and/or production of toxic materials, decrease your carbon emissions, and improve your design, construction, and packaging. In addition, the site provides profiles of companies that have achieved success in sustainable agriculture, renewable energy, zero-waste manufacturing, green building, independent retail, and community capital.

B Corporation (www.bcorporation.net) has developed a free and extraordinarily detailed survey designed to help business owners gauge where they stand in terms of practices (conducting business as though people matter, having a positive environmental footprint), profit (employee compensation, charitable giving), and products (how beneficial they are, how they are produced and packaged). The survey is tailored to the size and revenue of your company and adjusts its criteria and information depending upon your industry, whether you're in consumer goods, finance, insurance, health care, industrial goods, raw materials, the service industry, or even utilities. You'll also find tool kits, lists of resources, templates, and examples of best practices embedded in the survey.

But what about the rest of us who aren't entrepreneurs or business owners? Even if you're not the boss, you can infuse your workplace with the idealist spirit. In a lot of cases, it's just a matter of picking up the phone or knocking on the right person's office door. If you work for a large corporation, there's likely to be someone in HR who coordinates a company team to Race for the Cure or participate in some other community-involvement initiative. They've done the legwork of providing access to charitable activities and setting up partnerships and policies to allow employees to bond and to fit volunteerism and philanthropy into their lives. Check your company's website or contact that HR person to find out how you can take advantage of what already exists.

If you'd like to launch a particular activity or charitable program, volunteer to help put it together. Laying the groundwork is always the hardest part of getting a service or philanthropic initiative started, and your contact will be a lot more likely to pay attention to your ideas if she doesn't feel like all the work will be heaped in her lap.

For help in setting up a service program at work, you could contact AngelPoints (www.angelpoints.com/home), a California-based software company that has developed a program to help companies start up and measure their CSR (corporate social responsibility) programs (more on CSR in Chapter 9). Another site that offers support services for volunteer programs at work is the Corporate Volunteer Works Program at Grassroots.org (www.grassroots.org/support/volunteers).

If you're interested in helping your company improve their resource efficiency, you might try contacting the Rocky Mountain Institute (http://rmi.org/sitepages/pid55.php). The Taproot Foundation (www.taprootfoundation.org) can offer help in setting up a skilled volunteer program.

BSR.org is a consultancy that helps global companies develop social responsibility practices with regard in particular to the environment and human rights.

I'm discovering a conscience but I haven't been a charitable person until recently (though during a charity week in college I raised $300 by walking across hot coals). Once a year our paper does a charity issue where we auction off a load of stuff and donate the proceeds to a nonprofit. I had followed the role of Sisters of the Road in advocating against a controversial law outlawing sitting or lying on the sidewalk, saying it was unfairly targeting homeless people. The integrity of their stand on the issue, when other nonprofits seemed to be playing politics, impressed me. The [paper's charity] committee got together to discuss which charity could best use the money. I just kept arguing harder than anyone else to give it to Sisters of the Road. I was really pleased that my passion

If you work for a small organization, engaging the company and its employees in service or philanthropy may be entirely up to you. Regardless of where you're employed, we have a few ideas for how to build at the office enough interest in charitable and particularly volunteer programs that the company decides to make community involvement a priority.

1. Build Buzz. The best way to get others interested in volunteering is to start talking about your experience with any organization you're already involved with. When you're having lunch with colleagues or sharing a ride with your boss to a client meeting, tell stories about your volunteer work or board service. Post fliers on your office door or the wall of your cube, or even near the coffeepot, announcing any events sponsored by your organizations, with a casual handwritten note on the bottom inviting anyone who would like to learn more to call you or come by your desk. If you volunteer with artisans or children, display their wares or artwork around your office—they will be great conversation starters that will inevitably lead to a chance to talk about the nonprofit. By sharing your experience in this low-pressure, casual way, you'll plant the idealist seed in people's minds. After all, they may realize, if you can do it, why can't they? If someone tells you how much they admire your efforts and expresses amazement that you're able to carve out the time to do it, invite them to join you one day so they can see for themselves how much good can be done from minimal effort.

If you're not already involved with a nonprofit but would like to see your company do more for the local or global community, your best bet would be to research organizations that could benefit from the product or service your company sells or provides. For example, Aetna's AERO program (Aetna Employees Reaching Out) provides opportunities for employees to develop educational programs surrounding organ and tissue donation; in Greensboro, North Carolina, volunteers with American Express's Junior Achievement program go to K–12 classrooms to talk about financial literacy, workforce preparedness, ethics, and business and economics; AAA of Northern California, Nevada, and Utah organizes safety-related activities such as installing car seats for children, park and beach cleanups, and health-related charity walks. Making natural matches between your company and a cause will not only make it easier for individuals to see how they can personally affect a nonprofit, it will serve you well if and when you decide to attempt to engage a broader swath of employees in donating their time, skills, or money.

Unfortunately, there's no eBay for the nonprofit world that allows companies to do an easy search for an organization that might need their resources. You are just going to have to invest time in the search. But it won't be a ton of time. Let's say you work for a company that makes baby clothes. You can start by going to Idealist.org and doing a database search for an organization that serves infants in your area. That will take you maybe five minutes. Say you find three or four that match your criteria. Then you might evaluate their financial health through Guidestar, Charity Navigator, or Idealist.org. Next, you could use local networks. It would probably take you just an hour or two to use local networks to find individuals or organizations who have dealt with these groups. Maybe these nonprofits are mentioned on blogs or in the newspaper or magazines. Once you pinpoint the one that has the best reputation and would be a good fit for your company, give them a call. Do a site visit. Maybe volunteer once yourself to see how well organized they are and whether you think your employees would feel comfortable there. You'll know when you've found the right organization. It'll feel right, and finding it will have taken very little time.

2. *Get People Invested.* Let's say you've done a great job building buzz and now you've got a group of people interested in learning more about your nonprofit and what you do for it. The next best step would be to invite them to join you for a group volunteer project. It's crucial that their first experience with the nonprofit be a success, so as you plan the event, remember to:

Make it personal. Before setting up the first project, send out an email or create a Web survey asking colleagues what they'd like to do. More important, ask them what skills they would like to use or learn. In this way, you position your activity not only as a charitable act, but as an experience that could benefit the volunteers in the long run. The more relevant and personally rewarding your project is, the better your shot at getting your group hooked on volunteering.

Make it fun. If you start out suggesting a project that requires too much training or places a burden on the company to provide resources, you may overwhelm or intimidate your fledgling volunteers. Now is not the time to suggest a visit to the hospice, even if you work for a medical supply company. Make your first project accessible. (Environmental issues, for example, are often easier to get people involved in.)

You can look on page 84 for ideas on where to find independent or company-sponsored group activities. Propose a fun weekend project that involves employees and their families—often people don't join because they don't want to sacrifice their family time (look to page 86, for family-friendly project suggestions).

Make the good feelings last. After every project, make sure to follow up with the group. You can do this by email, or suggest everyone get together for lunch to talk about the experience. Regardless, make sure that you explain why the project mattered and remind them all what the end results were, such as, "Because of your efforts, four families are now living in safe, sturdy new homes." Talk about what you'd like to do next time and ask if anyone has suggestions as to how to make another project even more successful or relevant to what that person would like to accomplish professionally. The more invested

people are in the process, the more they'll be eager to participate in future opportunities.

3. Demonstrate Success. Since your ultimate goal is to convince
your company to incorporate community involvement—
whether as a formal volunteer program or a philanthropic part-
nership—into their business practice, you'll want to document
how your group's efforts have benefited not only the community, but also the employees. Over a period of six months, for
example, keep track of everyone's time or skill contributions,
and take note of how these activities have improved teamwork
or morale. If any activities take place during the lunch hour,
make sure to point out that the workday didn't suffer, that
company funds weren't spent, and that employees still man-
aged to do their jobs. In addition, gather research about other
companies that have implemented community service or philanthropic programs and how they have benefited. Important
points you can make:

- Employers who provide opportunities for volunteerism
  show higher rates of employee retention, morale, and
  pride in the company
- Companies that contribute service or engage in
  philanthropy can take advantage of the resulting free
  positive PR
- Allowing volunteers to represent the company in the
  community can open doors to new markets for your
  product or service

4. *Do the Thinking for Them.* Let's say that you've had a great response to your group volunteer projects, so much that you've had to break your coworkers into smaller groups to accommodate everyone. As grateful as everyone is to you for doing all the work, they're starting to question why the company itself doesn't sponsor community service projects. Now you've got enough groundswell to take your cause higher up the executive ladder. Once you have all your evidence in hand, you can make a formal presentation to your boss or HR director (if you work for a medium to large business) or the manager, founder, or owner (if you work for a small one) to make them see how it behooves them to support the charitable efforts of employees. Your goal will be to present the evidence that enough employees are interested in service to warrant the company setting up a community involvement program.

It's possible that the HR director won't know what setting up such a program would entail or exactly what it would look like, so come to your meeting prepared to describe programs other companies have successfully adopted. You can go to the Business Alliance for Local Living Economies (www.livingeconomies.org)

website for terrific examples of how some small- and medium-size companies are toeing the triple bottom line (measuring success in terms of having positive impacts on people, the planet, and profit). There is also no reason why you can't look to a larger company for inspiration and tailor it to your company's capabilities. Some of the most heralded programs in the country, drawn from the winners of the Points of Light Foundation's 2006 and 2007 Awards for Excellence in Workplace Volunteering, include:

- Citi's "Teach Children to Save" and "Get Smart About Credit" financial education programs. Citi also encourages all employees to take a paid day off to volunteer for the nonprofit of their choice.
- McGraw-Hill's Writers to the Rescue initiative, which matches editors, writers, PR specialists, graphic designers, web developers, and marketers with nonprofits who need help creating or fine-tuning their communications efforts, such as developing web content, editing grant proposals, or writing promotional materials.
- UPS's Neighbor to Neighbor program, founded on the idea that UPS drivers and employees are first-hand witnesses to the immediate needs of individual communities. Each district has a coordinator to help employees match their interests and skills to a variety of volunteer projects as well as board service opportunities.

We'd like to point out that none of these examples are from technology companies. The technology industry is uniquely suited for volunteerism, especially virtual and skilled. Most nonprofits just don't have the time or specialization to implement certain technological advances, programs, or practices, even though they know such an investment would improve their reach and their efficiency, and companies who specialize in tech can offer a lot of help in this arena with very little effort. But as the above examples prove, not to mention other companies, such as Timberland, Gap, Home Depot, Starbucks, and the Walt Disney Company, it's not just tech businesses that can develop outstanding employee volunteer and philanthropic programs.

5. Be Open to Different Levels of Support. Your company may not be willing to implement a community service program, but they might be willing to make a donation or sponsor a volunteer day once a quarter. In other words, take what you can get. Give the nonprofit you're working with, the company that employs you, and your team time to get to know one another and reap the rewards of their relationship. In time, the company may see fit to increase their involvement with your cause.

EVERYONE'S BEST INTEREST

As we've pointed out, implementing community involvement or philanthropic programs is great for employees. It can provide opportunities for skill improvement, team building, and morale boosts, and enhance overall employee retention, pride, and satisfaction. These programs are also good for companies. Odds are a good manager will see the overall benefits such a program can have to his company in the form of morale, PR, visibility, and other long-term benefits. But maybe you're just not sure you can afford the investment if you're a business owner, or maybe the company you work for is still dragging its heels, despite your best efforts.

If your company still needs convincing, one last thing you can try is the "everyone else is doing it" approach. You can tell them about a concept and business practice called corporate social responsibility that is gaining momentum in companies throughout the country, a result of converging forces that may be permanently blurring some of the lines between corporate and nonprofit America. Understanding those forces and how they are shaping the way we live and work will help you bolster your case for launching a volunteer or philanthropic or even recycling program in your current workplace. After all, you'll be able to point out, if the competition is doing it, shouldn't we?

IDEALISM IN ACTION

BEING FOCUSED ON WHAT YOU WANT REALLY HELPS YOU DRIVE FORWARD. I WAS VERY FOCUSED ON WANTING TO HELP PEOPLE AND USING YAHOO!'S RESOURCES. DAVID FILO [COFOUNDER OF YAHOO!] SAID THE MOST IMPRESSIVE THING ABOUT ME WAS MY PERSISTENCE. I WOULD BUG HIM EVERY WEEK ON THE SAME DAY AT THE SAME TIME AND HE FINALLY JUST CAVED. HE'S A

BUSY GUY; GETTING A RESPONSE OUT OF SOMEONE WHO IS THAT BUSY IS JUST IMPOSSIBLE. SO I JUST LEFT HIM IMS AND MESSAGES, AND WHEN I FINALLY CAUGHT UP WITH HIM HE SAID, "THANK YOU FOR BEING SO PERSISTENT."

YOU'VE GOT TO HAVE PASSION, LOVE FOR WHAT YOU DO, AND BE WILLING TO REDESIGN YOUR PLAN. I'VE RARELY SEEN THINGS WORK JUST THE WAY I WANT THEM TO, AND WHEN THEY DO [THE RESULT] IS USUALLY NOT AS GOOD AS WHEN I SPEND TIME STRUGGLING WITH IT. GO BACK TO THE DRAWING BOARD, LET GO OF YOUR EGO, DON'T BURN YOUR BRIDGES. A LOT OF PEOPLE TRY TO GO THROUGH THINGS THE CRUSADE ROUTE AND THAT RARELY WORKS.

THERE'S A TRICK TO BUILDING ANYTHING: REMEMBER WHAT YOUR INTENT IS. AM I INTENDING TO MAKE AN OMELET TODAY? SOMETIMES YOU MAKE SCRAMBLED EGGS, BUT IF YOU HOLD YOUR FOCUS OF MAKING AN OMELET, YOU'RE GOING TO HAVE AN OMELET AT THE END OF THE PROCESS. HAVING FOCUS, KNOWING WHAT YOU WANT TO DO, THE COMMUNITY THAT YOU WANT TO SERVE, AND UNDERSTANDING WHO YOU'RE WORKING WITH—ONCE YOU HAVE ALL THOSE FACTORS, AND THE RANDOM FACTORS ALIGN, YOU'RE DONE.

—James Jones, former Yahoo! employee, employee volunteer, visionary and co-architect for several Yahoo! for Good projects, including serving at the Houston Astrodome and helping to create the computer program that reunited families in Houston following Hurricane Katrina.

Everything You Need to Know About Corporate Social Responsibility

9

Corporate social responsibility (CSR) involves companies paying attention and taking responsibility for the effects their business strategies and products have on the outside world. This is a relatively new concept, yet it's an idea that is spreading quickly as society changes its expectations of the role businesses should play and their obligation to the community. Well, what's new about that, you may ask. What's new is that, perhaps for the first time, the pressure to change is not coming from a few outside protesters; it's often coming from within—many businesses are changing what they expect of themselves. We see evidence of this progressiveness in the number of companies that have made it easy for their employees to contribute to local and even global communities and causes through programs that partner with nonprofits. Almost every major business school in the country offers classes in social responsibility. In addition, entrepreneurs are launching an increasing number of new companies, often called "hybrids" or "for-benefit companies," with the double goal of creating profit and providing benefits to society.

Companies that incorporate principles of CSR prove that profit, efficiency, good customer service, and productivity don't have to be at odds with sustainability, generosity, compassion, and social justice. And that's good news for an idealist like you.

> As of 2007, there is about $2.3 trillion invested in socially responsible U.S. companies. That's an increase of more than 18 percent since 2005, almost one out of every nine dollars.[5]

WHY SHOULD CSR MATTER TO ME?

There are a few reasons to learn more about CSR. If you're a business owner or manager, it's in your best interest to see how other companies have benefited by adopting socially responsible principles. If you're considering trying socially responsible investing, learning to identify companies who follow CSR principles might be of interest to you. If you think you might soon be looking for a new job, the information that follows will help you recognize the hallmarks of a company actively putting social responsibility into practice. And last, if you're eager to find ways to work for good through your workplace—the main focus of this and the previous chapter—knowing how and why other companies have set up programs that incorporate a do-good philosophy into their business may help you convince your employer to do the same. In this final way, perhaps, we can create environments in which idealists who also happen to be office managers, pizza deliverers, executive assistants, human resource directors, accountants, designers, engineers, IT specialists, pastry chefs, concierges, dog groomers, salespersons, publicists, market researchers, real estate analysts, project managers, or any other job title you can think of, will no longer need to leave their beliefs and values at the door when they walk into their workplace.

To make this new work environment a reality, however, you'll need to be able to rebut arguments that CSR isn't worthwhile or doesn't work. So let's begin by explaining how and why a growing number of businesses are paying attention to corporate social responsibility, and enjoying success because of it.

A LITTLE HISTORY

Until recently, we've lived in a world where capitalism and social responsibility were treated as mutually exclusive. Perhaps the most famous analysis of this divide, one still referred to in modern-day debates, was summarized by Milton Friedman in 1970 in a famous *New York Times Magazine* article called "The Social Responsibility of Business Is to Increase Its Profits." In it, he made the case that a business's business is, well, business. That's what it's good at, that's what it should focus on. To ask business leaders to divert their attention away from serving the market and making money for shareholders is to sabotage the business and capitulate to socialism. Yet *Business Ethics* editor and publisher Marjorie Kelly writes, "Good corporate citizenship is a superior form of management . . . It simply makes sense:

managing a company for one measure alone—shareholder value—is like flying a 747 solely for maximum speed. You can shake the plane apart in the process."[6]

History seems to have proven Ms. Kelly right. It would seem that the traditional rules of the capitalist game can encourage our most selfish, most mercenary tendencies; some companies have been torn apart because there's always someone, somewhere, willing to bend the rules to pad the profit margin. Friedman and other skeptics of CSR believe the laws we have in place to force companies to adhere to certain standards of safety and ethical behavior are enough to keep most companies safe, and that we should leave the federal government to apply them to prevent harm to society. The problem, say pro-CSR supporters, is that doing so is a reactive measure, demanding change only after the damage has been done.

An environment in which a spirit of service, taking the form of volunteerism, philanthropy, community involvement, or yes, social responsibility, is allowed to flourish is also one that may have a better chance at avoiding many of the pitfalls that can trip up a company. That's good for the business, of course, but it's also good for employees.

> **Lest you get the idea that we idealists are anti-business, we want to make it clear that we know that most companies abide by the law. Most people who build businesses are anxious to leave behind a positive legacy, and they do. Entrepreneurs and business leaders are a creative force of our country, creating jobs, wealth, opportunity, and innovation. The concept of corporate social responsibility, however, takes the idea of business as a force for good to a new level.**

CSR DEFINED, SORT OF

Before we get into the details of what a company or employee can accomplish through CSR, it would be appropriate to offer a precise, universally agreed-upon definition. Except there isn't one yet. We think this is because few people can agree fully on what constitutes "socially responsible" behavior. Is a company embracing the concept of CSR if it makes generous contributions to social causes yet ignores its environmental impact? Can a company make a product some might consider harmful to society, such as cigarettes, noisy motorcycles, or fatty doughnuts, and also embody CSR philosophy? These are good questions, ones that we believe deserve to be debated, though not in this book.

> There are many websites, like CSR Wire (www.csrwire.com) and Net Impact (www.netimpact.org/index.cfm), and books, like *What Matters Most* by Jeffrey Hollender, that examine why CSR is a good thing, but to read a more diverse set of opinions on the subject, simply Google "corporate social responsibility" and you'll find hundreds of articles analyzing its pros and cons.

While we can't tell you precisely what constitutes a company that follows CSR, there are two constants you will see in any business that defines itself as such:

1. *Stepping up to the social responsibility plate is voluntary.* Of course there is already legislation in place to prevent

obvious abuses of human or civil rights or destruction of the environment, and most companies follow those laws to the letter. But a company that identifies itself as practicing CSR works toward eliminating those injustices and others by going above and beyond anything the government, and sometimes even the public, demands. Their business practice has nothing to do with legislation, and everything to do with doing what's right simply because it's the right thing to do. In more and more cases, this philosophy is folded into the company's overall mission and vision.

2. *While business has to be good for society, it still has to be good for business.* What this means is that profit is still the point—without it the company can't thrive and ultimately contribute the good that it would like to do. Some critics assert that companies that toot the CSR horn are simply following consumer trends. That may be so, but it will be interesting to see which nascent socially responsible business and management practices, instigated to appeal to consumer trends, ultimately become industry standards.

WHY NOW?

We can't strictly define CSR, and we can't even guarantee that the philosophy behind corporate social responsibility is going to become the corporate standard (though we suspect it will). So why do we think it's so important you understand the concept now?

Because More People (Including You) Care How the Game Is Played

In his book *Capitalism and Freedom*, Milton Friedman wrote, "There is one and only one social responsibility of business—to use its resources and engage in activities designed to increase its profits so long as it stays within the rules of the game."[7] Well, now more people are asking, why not change the rules of this game? Why not adjust our capitalist focus from one exclusively on shareholder value—benefiting those who own a piece of the business—to one that encompasses stakeholder value—benefiting anyone directly or indirectly affected by an organization's or company's actions? Capitalism *and* charity, profit *and* philanthropy, value *and* volunteerism.

Because Social Responsibility Is a Competitive Asset

The rules of capitalism can be revisited based on the results of research conducted in the thirty years since Friedman's article. For example, in 2002, a DePaul University study revealed that the overall financial performance of the companies that landed on the 2001 *Business Ethics* Best Citizen list was actually better than that of other companies on the S&P 500 index.[8] The most comprehensive study to date, in 2003, conducted an analysis of more than thirty years of all the known studies examining the relationship between corporate financial performance (CFP) and corporate social performance (CSP) and concluded

BLEACHING THE BEE'S KNEES

Most people don't think "green" when they think about bleach, yet in 2008 Clorox bought Burt's Bees, the natural personal care company, to serve as the poster child for its new eco-friendly initiative and line of products. Is Clorox serious about turning over a new environmentally responsible leaf, or is it simply jumping on the green bandwagon to keep up with the latest trend? It's too soon to tell (and regardless we wouldn't presume to judge). But as John Replogle, chief executive of Burt's Bees, told concerned customers when they called Clorox headquarters following the acquisition, "Don't judge Clorox as much by where they've been as much as where they intend to go." Clorox claims that by its one-hundredth anniversary in 2013, many more of its products will have gone green.

The joining of Clorox and Burt's Bees is an example of the potential dilemmas and opportunities inherent in developing businesses that achieve the two constants mentioned on pages 189–190. In the press release distributed announcing the purchase, Beth Springer, Clorox's executive vice president of strategy and growth, said, "Burt's Bees has a highly effective strategy and plan, strong trade practices and organizational capabilities, and a robust culture and esprit de corps that we want to leverage and protect. We strongly believe Clorox's deep capabilities to drive demand creation . . . coupled with Burt's Bees' strong heritage of innovation to delight consumers, create a right to win."

That's business-speak for, we want to keep what's good about Burt's Bees and use our resources to increase its reach and earning potential. True to the mission of socially responsible business, this arrangement should benefit stakeholders and shareholders alike. Sounds good to us. Time will tell if Clorox and Burt's Bees each hold up their end of the CSR bargain.

that there appears to be a "virtuous cycle" between the two—strong CSP begets strong CFP, and strong CFP allows companies to spend more on strengthening their CSP initiatives.[9] In short, companies that adopt socially responsible (and to a lesser degree, environmentally responsible) programs and initiatives continue to be profitable and experience growth.

How can it be that companies that don't exclusively focus on generating the greatest amount of wealth possible for their shareholders can compete with companies that do? There are a few possible explanations:

1. Reputation counts, especially in an age when the slightest misstep can be blasted on blogs for everyone to dissect. How a company is run, and the behavior and attitude of the people who run it, is up for scrutiny by the general public in a way that it couldn't be before the Internet. Also, more individuals now try to educate themselves about their investments and want to feel good about where they put their money. Shareholder satisfaction *and* stakeholder satisfaction matter in the long run.

2. The in-house monitoring required to achieve CSP means that managers are forced to pay better attention to all aspects of their business, which pays off in fewer production errors, better service, and improved efficiency.

3. According to the 2003 study, a company that gets high CSP ratings is more likely to receive endorsements from agencies such as the Environmental Pro-

tection Agency. With more consumers scrutinizing the labels of the products they bring into their homes, having such a label can add up to significant competitive advantage over another company.

4. Employees who believe they work for companies that are socially and environmentally responsible have consistently been shown to have better morale, which translates to lower turnover and therefore less money wasted on training and hiring costs, not to mention stronger intellectual capital.

All of these reasons will be valuable ammunition should you decide to push for CSR where you work.

BRINGING CSR INTO YOUR WORKPLACE

Though every year the number of companies actively incorporating CSR into their business model rises, most of us probably don't work for one of those companies. Yet before each of them started implementing their programs, someone had to spark the idea, start asking questions, and set the ball in motion. Why can't that someone be you?

Change comes from within. It's understandable that not everyone can work for a company that is perfectly aligned with their values, and we're not going to suggest that you jeopardize your paycheck to instigate change. But whether you're in the corner office or sharing a cubicle with another intern, remember that you have the power to inspire CSR. How? Because the one thing a person can do is ask the right questions. By simply putting your ideas out there, by voicing your concern, you open up the door to change. You may not get the answers or results you want, but maybe someone else will hear your questions and begin to question things themselves, and then maybe someone else will hear their questions, and so on and so forth, until enough people are demanding answers that those who are in power are forced to pay attention to, and maybe even take a second look at, how they do business.

Finding resources for how individuals can instigate social responsibility from within the workplace isn't easy, even for us, because most of what's been published is geared for corporations and written from a corporate angle. One excellent source for ideas and examples of how ordinary individuals can implement change from within, however, is an article by Debra Meyerson posted on the *Stanford Social Innovation Review* website and called "The Tempered Radicals: How Employees Push Their Companies—Little by Little—to Be More Socially Responsible" (www.ssireview.org/pdf/2004FA_feature_meyerson.pdf).

Whom should you talk to? It could be the leaders of your company, or your managers. It might be the Marketing Department, or even the comptroller. If it's not clear who is in charge of philanthropy and charity, ask around until you find the right person. Also, it's often good to speak to people who have been with the company for a long time. It's possible, for example, that they'll know whether any initiatives have already been attempted, but got dropped when the organizer left the company.

What kind of questions should you ask? It depends on where you work. If you work for a clothing manufacturer, for example, you might want to know more about how the clothes are made. Where are the factories? Who is monitoring them? What are the working conditions there? How does the final product get to the retailers? Are people paid a living wage at the retailers that sell the clothes? Do they get benefits? Almost any company that sells a product—coffee, food, apparel, toys, furniture, home improvement materials, electronics, cars, etc.—should be able to answer these questions. If they can't or won't, that might tell you something. Perhaps you need to get more people to ask the same questions to prove that the answers do matter, for all the reasons listed in the beginning of this chapter.

Let's say you work for an accounting firm or a company that sells services or advice. You might not consider yourself in an industry that "makes" something. Look around, though. The paper, the electricity, the cardboard sleeves on your colleagues' disposable coffee cups—offices are thought factories whose waste can be measured in carbon footprints and stacks of paper instead of industrial pollution. Environmental issues are some of the easiest ones to tackle on a small scale from within an office. You might ask if anyone has calculated how much wasted paper the office produces, or inquire about the energy bill. Is there a recycling program in place? If not, would anyone mind if you helped start one? Who supplies office materials, and has anyone considered looking into distributors who specialize in green products? What cleaning supplies does the company furnish the cleaning staff, or if it hires a cleaning service, is it one that uses environmentally sensitive products (not just for the sake of the environment but for the sake of the people breathing the fumes day in and day out)?

Regardless of where you work, you might ask HR what the company contributes annually in charitable donations. Does anyone know the employee giving rate?

Where do your colleagues volunteer? Ask if it would be OK for you to start a volunteer program, or ask if you can provide some resources to services that help companies set up volunteer or philanthropic programs.

> Change is happening on a professional level. I hear friends in the traditional corporate world saying, 'Hey, we're doing Hands-on Atlanta this weekend,' 'We're starting a carpooling network...' I think because it gets so much media attention, if someone were to bring an initiative to a manager, it's now a much more accepting environment. There's potential for people within organizational structures to impact in big and little ways.
>
> —David Murphy, CEO, Better World Books; Atlanta, Georgia

Yeah, Right!

You might be thinking, "There's no way I can go into the boss's office or corporate headquarters and ask this stuff!" Well, most people aren't quite ready for their Erin Brockovich moment, it's true. But success is all in the way you ask and frame the questions. Don't accuse. Don't point fingers. Don't assume you know the answers. Don't judge! And you probably don't even want to mention the words "corporate social responsibility." Maybe you'll be having a casual talk with your manager and find the opportunity to say something like "I've been thinking more about my place in the world and I'd really like to know more about how the company I work for feels about these issues. Do you know? Can you tell me who might?" If you approach the subject in a nonaggressive way, your manager is likely to point you in the right direction. In addition, now you've shared your concerns with another person, who may start thinking, "Hey, what about my place in the world?" He may decide the answers to your questions matter to him, too.

INSPIRING CSR BEFORE YOU JOIN THE WORKPLACE

If working for a company that practices corporate social responsibility is important to you, then you should be sure to ask the right questions whenever you're interviewing for a new job. As a prospective employee, you have influence. Imagine if every idealist who interviewed for a position with a company asked the questions above, or even some of the following:

- What is this company's record on human rights? What was it ten years ago?
- What is this company's vision for how it intends to do business in the future? How does this differ from the way it has done business in the past?
- Has it established a recycling program? Is there anyone in charge of improving employee diversity?

- Does the company have a philanthropic or volunteer program? Would it be all right if I helped organize volunteer or philanthropic initiatives so long as it didn't interfere with my or anyone else's work?

Ideally you would ask these same questions of a variety of people connected to the business, such as someone in marketing, in human resources, and a random employee. In this way you can get the company line but also find out how people not tied to the company line answer the questions.

IDENTIFYING SOCIALLY RESPONSIBLE BUSINESSES

Even if an employee, job hunter, or investor/philanthropist asks all the right questions, how can she know if a company really practices CSR or just has a crackerjack PR team who knows how to spin the facts? It's tricky. As we've reiterated, there are no fixed standards as to what constitutes true socially responsible business practices.

But information is often out there if you know where to look. Whether you're curious to know how your own company stacks up against others, looking for a good investment, or if you're thinking of changing jobs and would like to apply to companies with socially responsible reputations, the following steps should give you the tools with which to gauge a company's commitment to CSR.

Seek Out For-Benefit Companies

If you're serious about identifying companies with strong commitments to CSR, your best place to start is by focusing on for-benefit companies, also known as hybrids, stakeholder corporations, or triple-bottom-line companies, whose raison d'être is to make money and simultaneously provide a benefit to society. As we discussed in Chapter 2, for-benefit companies are a fast-growing segment of the business market. Many of these businesses are members of an organization called the Social Venture Network (www.svn.org).

Sometimes the corporate world responds to what we're doing as 'Isn't that cute, isn't that nice that they're doing something for the world...' But we're in a brutally competitive market. We're everything a business is. We're pure capitalism, but at the same time our core mission is not solely stockholder return or about how much money we can make, but making a difference through literacy, education, and environmental stewardship. In terms of what happens every day, and the challenges the business provides, and the rush, it's all there and then some.

Some well-known for-benefit or hybrid companies include Stonyfield Farm, The Body Shop, Tom's of Maine, Working Assets, Altrushare Securities, Clif Bar, Newman's Own, Odwalla, and Patagonia. Other less well-known but equally impressive companies are listed on the *Fast Company* Social Capitalist Awards list, which is usually reserved for nonprofits but which honored ten for-benefit companies in 2008:

Better World Books
Developing World Markets
Domini Social Investments
Equal Exchange
Herman Miller
New Leaf Paper
Organic Valley Family of Farms
Seventh Generation
ShoreBank
SustainAbility

Read the Lists

There are two well-established lists published every year that are generally considered trustworthy sources for the gold standards of corporate responsibility.

FORTUNE MAGAZINE 100 MOST ADMIRED COMPANIES

In recent years, the following companies have been in the top five in the Social Responsibility category (http://cgi.money.cnn.com/tools/fortune/most_admired.jsp):

Fortune Brands
International Paper
Starbucks
United Parcel Service
Walt Disney

BUSINESS ETHICS 100 BEST CORPORATE CITIZENS

In recent years, the following companies have been in the top five (www.business-ethics.com/node/75):

Advanced Micro Devices, Inc.
Green Mountain Coffee Roasters, Inc.
Intel Corporation
Motorola, Inc.
Nike, Inc.

In addition, *Business Ethics* publishes the Business Ethics Awards in the categories of corporate responsibility management, environmental sustainability, stakeholder accountability, and general excellence (www.business-ethics.com/BEAwards_all). While the Best Corporate Citizen's list is dominated by big business, the criteria for the Ethics Awards allow more medium and small companies to qualify for consideration. Therefore, past winners have included small publisher Berrett-Koehler in San Francisco, South Mountain Company (a build/design firm) on Martha's Vineyard, and the Weaver Street Market in North Carolina.

Be Aware of Online Sustainability Reports

There are a number of organizations online that have established benchmarks for sustainability, and ideally we would encourage you to read their reports. Unfortunately, most of these sites are geared toward analysts, journalists, researchers, and investors, and require significant fees to access these documents. If you have the funds to spend on downloading them, they are well worth it. If not, there are ways to use what information you can find there that's free.

With regard to any of these sites, there's one caveat. Though these organizations have taken great pains to set up objective measurable standards and stay clear of any obvious agenda, make no mistake about it, the agenda exists for the listing organization and for the companies that are listed. Every assessing organization judges corporate social responsibility through its own selective lens. That is, each one has a top priority, be it human rights, diversity, the environment, or one of any number of causes. None has established an assessment tool that can measure a company's performance in all of these arenas. And you will seldom find any that focus on the level of a company's volunteerism or community engagement.

So why bother? The fact that these companies are willing to pay a fee and be vetted to be listed on these sites marks a significant financial commitment to establishing themselves as a company that cares about CSR. Since a company is only going to spend money on what it believes will keep it solvent, healthy, popular, and positive in the public eye, the mere fact that they think it's important enough to be listed represents a huge step forward in the process of incorporating CSR into our capitalistic culture. Companies wouldn't bother investing in the process if getting mentioned on these lists didn't mean something to enough people to make a difference to their bottom line. Granted, only big, well-financed businesses can afford to be included in these lists, but if their socially responsible strategies prove to be successful, there's no reason why smaller companies won't follow in their footsteps when they can.

Some online sustainability reports worth knowing about:

CSRwire.com. The Corporate Social Responsibility Newswire is an excellent repository of information for anyone who wants to hear what global companies, agencies, NGOs, and other organizations have to say about their efforts to improve their socially responsible performance. That's right— what *they* have to say about themselves. These company-issued reports are free to read. The most valuable information the site has to offer, research and ratings provided by independent firms who analyze each company's performance on environmental, social, and governance (ESG) issues, is, unfortunately, restricted to anyone with about $500 to spare for each rating. So why do we recommend the site? Company reports, while certainly biased, are still worthwhile indicators of how seriously a company takes its commitment to change. The site also provides free access to articles about CSR, some research, and information about events promoting corporate social responsibility. We feel that until someone does provide free access to independent CSR ratings, this is a good way to get a quick preliminary overview about the company you may be researching.

Global Reporting Initiative. This nonprofit foundation (www .globalreporting.org) has compiled a sustainability reporting framework and guidelines that measure a company's economic, environmental, human rights, labor, product responsibility, and social performance. Ultimately, it feeds into the same reporting database as CSRwire.com, the Corporate Social Responsibility Newswire. If a company posts a sustainability report, you'll find it on this site.

Social Accountability International. SAI (www.sa-intl.org) advocates for the protection of human rights using a system designed to promote and manage ethical workplace conditions throughout the supply chain in companies around the world. They have also developed a workplace auditing system to measure these companies' social performance and to root out any disregard of labor laws. They don't offer an easily digested ratings report that would be useful to an individual looking for information about a particular industry or company, but they do provide an extensive list of websites that advocate for general labor and humanitarian issues, corporate social responsibility, and socially responsible investing.

UN Global Compact. This is the only one of these organizations that doesn't provide independent reports to measure sustainable behavior, but it is also the only one for which participation in their sustainability program is free. The Global Compact (www.unglobalcompact.org) was designed to help bridge the gap between the UN's mission of fostering peace, poverty reduction, and human rights, and a business's goals of profit and growth. Any company can join with the exception of what the site calls "micro-businesses," those with ten employees or fewer. As participants, companies promise to incorporate and support the values expressed in ten principles addressing corporate behavior regarding human rights, labor standards, the environment, and anticorruption. They post COPs (Communication on Progress), which outline the goals and strategies they have set regarding folding the ten principles into their business model and then list the measurable results of their activities. In this way, you can read that Crystal Windows and Doors Systems, Ltd., a construction and engineering firm based in Flushing, New York, sponsored a blood drive, fund-raised for a local library, invested in areas of rural China, and participated in programs designed to boost energy efficiency in its business practices and final products. Global Compact also provides a list of "notable COPs," which acknowledges particularly inspiring reports.

Better Business Bureau. Many locally owned, smaller businesses are members of the BBB. The BBB will list reports for accredited and non-accredited businesses. Accredited businesses, of course, have paid a membership fee to be evaluated. If you see that the company is accredited, it means that the bureau has reviewed company policy and practice according to BBB standards and deemed it ethical and honest. A quick search in the reports for local or national companies in the United States and Canada will tell you immediately if a company has received an unusual number of complaints against it or been involved in any legal arbitration, a sign that perhaps you should research the company a little more closely.

Nobody's Perfect

It's possible to get frustrated as you start discovering what companies do and don't do regarding issues that matter to you, whether it's the environment, human rights, donations, or even diversity. No company is perfect. Clorox, as we have seen, is making strides to improve its environmental record, but some people may not be able to get past the company's earlier history. Pfizer made $1.7 billion in product donations in 2006 and has implemented one of the best international volunteer programs in the country, but it does perform animal testing and conducts stem cell research. As usual, it will be up to you to decide which issues are most important to you, and to find the companies that best represent your values and that you believe are making the greatest difference.

MOVING FORWARD

A good paycheck, a stimulating work environment, challenging projects, generous benefits—sometimes these crucial elements to job satisfaction and career advancement have to take priority over our ideals. But that doesn't mean that we can't act upon our ideals while on the job or pursuing our career goals. Advocating for CSR within your current workplace, asking questions when interviewing for a new job, making socially responsible investments, supporting or even launching companies that make CSR the fulcrum of their business model—all of these are ways in which individuals can make a tremendous difference in the workplace, the community, and the world. Over the past thirty years activists have taken sneaker companies to task for violating human rights, oil and gas companies for spoiling the environment, Wall Street firms for their lack of diversity. These issues, once hardly a blip on the general public's radar, are now part of the national dialogue, and addressing them has become standard business practice for millions of companies. The tremendous progress that corporate America has made in tackling these complex problems is proof of how much can be accomplished when idealists take action.

IDEALISM IN ACTION

THE MISSION STATEMENT OF ROCK BOTTOM RESTAURANTS, INC., IS "TO RUN GREAT RESTAURANTS . . . FOR THE BENEFIT OF OUR GUESTS, OUR COMMUNITY, AND OURSELVES," SO IT REALLY WAS ONLY A MATTER OF TIME UNTIL SOMETHING HAPPENED; IT JUST HAPPENED FASTER THAN ANYONE THOUGHT. OUR HAND WAS FORCED WHEN WE TOOK OVER A REALLY HUGE OLD WAREHOUSE BY COORS FIELD, WHERE WE BUILT OUR

FIRST EVER CHOPHOUSE. THIS WAREHOUSE HAD BEEN HOME TO A NUMBER OF HOMELESS PEOPLE, AND WE FELT AWFUL THAT WE WERE DISPLACING THESE PEOPLE FOR OUR RESTAURANT. WE INVITED THEM TO DINNER FOR CHRISTMAS, MAYBE ABOUT FIFTY FAMILIES, AND WE CONTINUED TO DO THAT EVERY YEAR. IT'S NOT A BUFFET LINE LIKE IN A SOUP KITCHEN—THERE'S CHINA, REAL SILVERWARE, LINEN NAPKINS. EVENTUALLY MORE AND MORE PEOPLE STARTED TO COME, AND ONE CHRISTMAS EVE THE CAPTAIN OF THE AVALANCHE [DENVER'S HOCKEY TEAM], JOE SAKIC, SAID, "I THOUGHT YOU WERE CLOSED FOR CHRISTMAS."

WE SAID, "WE ARE, BUT WE'RE OPEN FOR THIS."

HE SAID, "WOW, THAT'S REALLY SPECIAL."

JOE AND HIS WIFE TOOK THEIR SUVS DOWN TO TOYS 'R' US AND FILLED UP TWO CARLOADS FULL OF TOYS. THE FOLLOWING YEAR THEY GAVE US A CHECK SO WE COULD BUY THE TOYS IN HIS NAME. FOLLOWING THAT, HIS CPA CALLED US AND ASKED US IF WE HAD THE PAPERWORK ALLOWING US TO BE A NONPROFIT. WE DIDN'T. THUS BEGAN THE PROCESS OF GETTING REGISTERED WITH THE IRS, AND THE FOUNDATION WAS BORN SO WE COULD EXPAND THESE HOLIDAY DINNER EVENTS. WE WERE IN SIXTEEN CITIES LAST YEAR, THIS YEAR WE'RE ADDING TWO MORE. THE CHOPHOUSE RESTAURANT WAS LOCATED ON 19TH STREET, AND JOE SAKIC'S NUMBER FOR THE AVALANCHE IS 19. THUS THE NAME, MIRACLE ON 19TH STREET.

—Jessica Newman, executive director, Rock Bottom Foundation; Louisville, Colorado

10

Changing the World and
Getting Paid to Do It

*I had a good-paying job but I couldn't stand my cubicle. 'It was
a great opportunity,' as my professors liked to remind me, but
I wasn't passionate about the work. Every day that I sat in
the cubicle I wanted to be somewhere else; I would have wild
daydreams about the things I would do with my life if... Then
one day I just stopped saying if.*

—MATT HOLTON, MICROBUSINESS PROGRAM COORDINATOR,
WILLAMETTE NEIGHBORHOOD HOUSING SERVICES;
CORVALLIS, OREGON

As we've seen, it doesn't take much to make the world a better place. Bringing canned goods to a food drive for the hungry, checking in on an elderly neighbor, organizing a fund-raiser, cleaning up a playground, serving as a board member, donating blood, mentoring a student, providing your skills pro bono, inspiring corporate social responsibility in your workplace, or contributing money to a cause close to your heart—all of these acts of giving, even the seemingly small ones, make a real difference.

Still, you might wish you could do more.

Imagine what it would feel like to make that contribution every day, to devote your talents and energy and professional skill and training toward promoting a cause that you fiercely believe in—and get paid to do it. How would it feel to build a career around working to make someone's life better, or to clean up the environment, or to push for the rights of a group that can't fight for itself? Full- or part-time, a job with a non-profit can be an ideal position where you get paid while having the opportunity to learn and grow and join forces with a team of passionate colleagues to change the world in a way you think works.

The nonprofit world is populated by individuals from all walks of life with all levels of education and professional experience. Some start out with a lifetime of service under their belts; others use the job as a means to incorporate service into their lives. Many people will say they never considered working for any company other than a nonprofit; others are "switchers," people who decided mid-career that the corporate world didn't offer them the opportunities or satisfaction they believed they could get with a nonprofit. Then there are the increasing droves of employees coming from the ranks of recent retirees, individuals who were happy to leave behind their old careers yet not quite ready, given financial needs or a desire for new challenges, for a life of full-time leisure. The information we offer in the following pages should be relevant regardless of where you fall in this vast spectrum.

Laying the groundwork for a successful job search looks much the same whether you're interested in a position with a nonprofit or a for-profit—except when it doesn't. In the following chapters, we'll explore various ways to help you identify the right position at the right organizations, as well as how to maximize your chances of landing your ideal nonprofit job.

But first, let's examine some of the misconceptions most people have about working for a nonprofit.

COMMON CONCERNS

"I'll starve."
"I'll never be able to support a family."
"I'll lose the professional respect of my peers."
"I'll have no stability."
"My friends and family won't understand; they'll think
   I'm wasting my potential."

If the idea of working for a nonprofit has ever crossed your mind, it's likely that one or even all of these fears have, too. And if you haven't already thought of any of them, someone in your family or circle of friends will probably bring up at least one or two the minute you mention the word "nonprofit." It's good to be aware of the downsides to any job, and these would be valid concerns—if they were true. Working to do good in the world does not mean a life of deprivation, nor is most of it much different from working elsewhere.

TOP TEN MYTHS OF WORKING FOR NONPROFIT ORGANIZATIONS

1. *No one makes any money.* While nonprofit salaries tend to top out sooner than they do in executive positions in the corporate world, nonprofit salaries are often similar to those in other industries. In addition, nonprofits often have excellent benefits packages and offer more generous vacation time than their corporate counterparts. The low pay also tends to be offset by the tremendous "psychic income" that accompanies doing a job you love.

2. *Nonprofits are a refuge for people who couldn't cut it in the business world.* Most people who work in nonprofits have chosen to be there. The vast majority of nonprofit employees and volunteers are intelligent, passionate people, many with graduate degrees and years of experience. In fact, defectors from the corporate world are often surprised to learn how difficult it is to make the transition into the nonprofit world, which has different, often rigorous standards of success.

   Some nonprofit leaders with for-profit backgrounds include:

   Joyce Roché, president and CEO, Girls Incorporated. Previous experience: president and COO of Carson, Inc; VP of global marketing at Avon Products, Inc.; 1998 *Business Week* "Top Manager to Watch"; named one of *Black Enterprise* magazine's "21 Women of Power and Influence in Corporate America" (1991) and one of their "40 Most Powerful Black Executives" (1994); awarded the *Black Enterprise* Legacy Award during their 2006 Women of Power Summit.

Judy Vredenburgh, president and CEO, Big Brothers Big Sisters of America. Previous experience: rose from buyer to executive management positions with several major retail corporations; executive vice president and general merchandise manager at Sizes Unlimited/Learner Woman; president and CEO of Chess King, a division of Melville Corporation.

Bill Novelli, CEO, AARP. Previous experience: began his career at Unilever, then cofounded and was president of Porter Novelli, now one of the world's largest public relations agencies and part of the Omnicom group; named one of the 100 most influential public relations professionals of the twentieth century by the industry's leading publication.

Marguerite Kondracke, president and CEO, America's Promise. Previous experience: founded the start-up Corporate Family Solutions (now Bright Horizons Family Solutions), the country's largest provider of workplace child care; named regional Entrepreneur of the Year by Ernst & Young.

3. *There's no upward mobility.* A common misperception is that people working in nonprofits are often taking a break or avoiding the "real" world where perfor mance reviews and end results are used as a benchmark for promotion and success. Nonprofits reward innovation, decisiveness, creativity, and professional excellence the same way their for-profit counterparts do. Many people switch between the nonprofit, government, and private sectors during their careers, but many also enjoy a lifetime of exciting and challenging work in nonprofits, rising up the ranks as their experience grows and positions become available. In fact, people in entry-level positions at nonprofits tend to enjoy earlier and more frequent leadership opportunities and responsibilities than in other sectors thanks to the less rigid hierarchical rules and fewer processes and layers within organizations.

Some high-profile young nonprofit leaders include:

Charissa Fernandez, 33, chief operating officer, The After-School Corp., New York City

Saramuthi Jayaraman, 32, co-director, Restaurant Opportunities Center United, New York City

Dionne Mack-Harvin, 35, executive director, Brooklyn Public Library, Brooklyn

Jeana Frazzini, 36, executive director, Basic Rights Oregon, Portland, Oregon

4. *Everyone who works in a nonprofit is nice.* Just because people choose to devote their work to a good cause doesn't mean that they are angels, and it certainly doesn't mean that they can't have a bad day. It's probably safe to say that as many people in the nonprofit sector are kind and friendly as in any other profession. In other words, most people are nice no matter where you work. But as in any job, the more passionate a person is about his goal, the more determined he is to make sure the job gets done, and gets done right. People who go into a nonprofit expecting everyone to be all smiles or expecting to receive endless pats on the back for doing their job are in for a rough time. The difficult personalities, big egos, and office politics that are well documented in more traditional professional environments exist in the nonprofit world, too. If anything, some people in nonprofits get a little too personally invested in their work, which can sometimes lead them to adopt a savior complex—when the cause and their particular solution to that cause become so important to them that they wind up judging others who don't get it or who have different ideas. This overemotional attachment can create severe rifts within nonprofits or weaken the organization's ability to partner with other agencies.

5. *Nonprofits aren't competitive.* The nonprofit sector can be as competitive and rigorous as any for-profit corporation. In a world of limited resources, nonprofit organizations compete intensely for media, recognition, funding, and the attention of a distracted public. Organizations collaborate often and talk about working together, but some organizations that provide similar services compete to be the most recognizable provider of that service. Groups sometimes feel they "own" an issue, believing that they do their work so effectively that they deserve to be a sort of brand name for the cause. For example, a group known for organizing marathons might bristle if another agency decides to sponsor one themselves. It can escalate into a sort of turf war, straining relationships and stymieing progress. In other situations, organizations tackle similar problems with different solutions. Think about how many organizations are working to reduce global warming, for example; every one of them has a specific way of approaching the problem. Then there are cases in which organizations have missions that are in direct opposition to one another, for example, highly polarizing issues such as abortion, environmental reform, or gun control.

6. *Nonprofits are inefficient, wasting time and money.* It's true that most nonprofits don't have clear bottom lines or profit margins, and in the case of organizations that promote awareness of an issue or encour-

age charity, it can be difficult to measure exactly how a human or environmental need has been served. In addition, limited resources can create situations in which client needs are often served at the cost of organizational maintenance. For example, a manager may be forced to choose between using funds to purchase more meals for people coming to the homeless shelter and using the money to train a volunteer manager. Difficult choices like this have to be made all the time, and not everyone will understand or approve of the final result, even going so far as to accuse the agency of inefficiency and disorganization. There are certainly some inefficient and disorganized nonprofits, just as there are plenty of dysfunctional organizations in the private sector. In neither case should these exceptions be considered a reflection on the sector as a whole.

7. *Nonprofit employees are constantly face-to-face with human suffering.* Nonprofits are formed because someone sees a wrong that needs to be made right, or a problem that needs to be solved. Much of nonprofit work involves direct hands-on involvement, and that can definitely take a strong stomach and nerves, whether you're working in a soup kitchen, for a mentoring program, on an abuse hotline, or fighting third world hunger. But many people who work for nonprofits are accountants, computer programmers, salespeople, human resource professionals, managers, fund-raisers, and executives. Many

more are researchers and advocates, acting as a support system for those performing direct service daily. There's a place for everyone to give to the best of his or her abilities.

8. *It's Birkenstocks and sweats, all the time.* Forget the hippie stereotype—cultures within nonprofits vary just like anywhere else. The corridors of a nonprofit hospital are filled with professionally dressed medical practitioners and administrators; universities allow for a hodgepodge of different styles, depending upon a person's role or rank; and at other large institutions with multimillion-dollar annual budgets business attire is often the norm, with many executives dressed in the conservative navy blue suits that are the norm in other corporate arenas.

9. *The nonprofit sector is mostly made up of left-wingers for left-wing causes.* The nonprofit sector itself does not have a political agenda, period. Organizations lean left, right, and everywhere in between. People of all worldviews are passionate about their issues. In addition, there are a significant number of faith-based organizations that may have conservative leanings and yet are deeply rooted in social justice causes, such as Habitat for Humanity, the Salvation Army, and many of the groups that are bringing hope and help to war-torn African countries.

10. *You may as well volunteer—it's pretty much the same thing.* This couldn't be more wrong. Nonprofits rely on volunteers to do much of their work, especially in

direct services. Anyone can volunteer, it's just a matter of making a good match. As crucial as volunteers are to the existence and advancement of a nonprofit, however, their role is necessarily limited. They are usually shielded from the organizational, financial, and other challenges with which the actual employees of a nonprofit must contend. A job in a nonprofit is at once more specialized and more broad-reaching than simple volunteer work, often requiring one to be manager, negotiator, writer, accountant, strategic thinker, and morale booster all at once. Whereas a volunteer who is well matched to her job will likely use one or two skills, most people working in nonprofits are forced to use management skills, negotiating skills, writing skills, financial acumen, strategic thinking—often all at once.

Working in a nonprofit comes with a unique set of opportunities and drawbacks, just like working in any other profession. Rich and diverse and dynamic, there's no better place for a person anxious to see what he or she is made of. It has unlimited rewards and unlimited challenges, just like all the best things worth pursuing.

I HAVE A CHECKERED PAST. I'VE WORKED FOR GOVERNMENT, FOR CORPORATE, FOR NONPROFITS. I WAS WORKING AT WELLS FARGO AND HAD BEEN TRANSFERRED TO SOUTHERN CALIFORNIA TO GET READY FOR AN UPCOMING ACQUISITION, AND IT BLEW UP. AFTER THAT I WAS GIVEN A CHANCE TO GO BACK TO SAN FRANCISCO AND WORK FOR WELLS OR STAY IN SOUTHERN CALIFORNIA AND TAKE A PACKAGE. I DID A LOT OF SEARCHING AND LOOKING AND DECIDED MY OWN BUSINESS WAS THE WAY TO GO. AN ANIMAL SHELTER WAS ONE OF MY CLIENTS. AS A CONSULTANT YOU GET LOTS OF JOB OFFERS, WHICH I USUALLY TURNED DOWN, BUT THE ANIMAL SHELTER SPOKE TO ME. I THOUGHT IT WOULD BE GREAT, WORKING WITH THE EMPLOYEES AND ANIMALS. BUT I DIDN'T UNDERSTAND HOW POLITICAL AND FRUSTRATING IT WOULD BE IN TERMS OF WORKING WITH ELECTED OFFICIALS. BECAUSE OF THE EXPERIENCE I HAD AS A CONSULTANT (I HAD ALSO TAUGHT AT UC IRVINE), I REALLY LIKED THE HIGHER EDUCATION ENVIRONMENT AND WORKING WITH STUDENTS. I THOUGHT IT WAS ONE OF THOSE AREAS WHERE IT WAS A FIT FOR ME. I STARTED A VERY SPECIFIC SEARCH FOR JOBS IN HIGHER EDUCATION AND WOUND UP HERE AT CLAREMONT AS A CAREER COUNSELOR. SINCE I'D HAD SO MANY CAREERS I THOUGHT I HAD SOMETHING TO OFFER.

IT'S NOT BETTER OR WORSE THAN CORPORATE, IT'S DIFFERENT. THERE IS NOTHING I REGRET, NOT A BIT. WHILE I GOT VALUE FROM MY BUSINESS, THERE'S SOMETHING MORE HERE, ASIDE FROM IT BEING A NONPROFIT AND FEELING THAT

EVERY DAY I HAVE AN IMPACT ON PEOPLE'S LIVES. IN ADDITION TO ALL THOSE WONDERFUL REWARDS, I HAVE A MUCH MORE PREDICTABLE KIND OF ENVIRONMENT. I COME HERE IN THE MORNING AND I HAVE AN IDEA OF WHAT I'M GOING TO DO, BUT THERE'S VARIETY. AND I'M ABLE TO LEAVE AT A DECENT HOUR OF THE DAY. I HAVE A FIVE-MINUTE COMMUTE, BUT EVEN IF I HAD A HALF-HOUR OR HOUR COMMUTE, THIS IS WHERE I'D WANT TO BE.

—Jackee Engles, Employer Relations, Office of Career Management, Claremont Graduate University; Claremont, California

11

The Search

As in any job pursuit, when applying for a position with a nonprofit, you'll want to write an impressive resume and cover letter and brush up on your interview technique. You don't need us to review the details of these important parts of the job-hunting process. If you're a student, your school certainly has a wide variety of resources available to you, and if you're switching from one career to another or have been out of the job market for a while, there are many excellent books out there that can give you clear guidance on how to begin (including our two free ebooks on the Idealist.org website, one for first-time or emerging professionals, *The Idealist Guide to Nonprofit Careers for First-Time Job Seekers* (www.idealist.org/en/career/guide/first time/index.html), and one for mid-career transitioners, *The Idealist Guide to Nonprofit Careers for Sector Switchers* (www.idealist .org/en/career/guide/sectorswitcher/index.html). What is less easy to find and what we'll provide here is an overview of what to expect as you travel down the nonprofit job-hunting path, and the best ways to maximize your chance of success. You'll find that many of the concepts and ideas we discussed in earlier chapters of this book also come into play during the nonprofit job hunt.

THE SEARCH—HOW IT LOOKS THE SAME

Remember how we said that a job search in the nonprofit world looks the same as one in the for-profit world, except when it doesn't? Let's talk a little more about that.

How will it look the same? To begin with, a nonprofit's standards will be just as high as those of any other business. Professionalism, competence, problem solving, attention to detail—these are the basic elements of good employee DNA, and they're going to matter here as much as they would anywhere else.

Second, if you want to shine, you'll have to do your research. When interviewing for a job, any job, knowledge is power. You already know that when meeting a company HR representative or prospective boss you need to show a solid working knowledge of the field. You're also aware that you should be prepared to prove you know something about the business and how it has recently performed. You make sure to indicate that you understand their products or services. You find a way to drop into your conversation how you'd like to help shape the department in which you'll be working, and maybe even reveal a familiarity with your prospective supervisor's job and accomplishments. You'll want to be equally prepared when interviewing for a job in a nonprofit. In the first two sections of this book we told you where to find the online resources you can use to load up on relevant information (and even if you can't get hard information about a particular organization, such as an annual report, you can arm yourself with material gleaned from websites and media that discuss the issue you are passionate about). The information in previous chapters of this book, particularly Chapter 4, will also prepare you to answer any questions about what unique skills, talents, and experience you have to offer.

Third, don't forget to talk the talk. Every profession has its own jargon. Book publishers talk about flap copy and first pass and signatures. Advertisers talk about bleeds and CRM and unique selling propositions. Familiarity with the lingo shows you're one of the tribe, so use it when you speak to anyone within the nonprofit world, especially in an interview. Don't set your interviewer's teeth on edge by referring to a nonprofit as a "company," because it will underscore just how much training you may need to fit in. (Someone with even limited experience already knows the difference between a company and a nonprofit.) Know what grants are and why they matter. If you're interested in a managerial position or even higher, get comfortable with fund-raising terminology and grant-writing techniques and media protocol. Just as you should dress for the job you want, you should speak like the job you want.

Last, as in the for-profit arena, the competition for jobs is intense. Job hunts are rarely easy, even for people with excellent qualifications and experience. Don't get discouraged if you don't get the first position you apply for. To stay ahead of the pack, particularly if you are new to the workforce, try not to pin all your hopes on working for the biggest and most famous nonprofits; be willing to investigate less well-known organizations that might not draw quite as many applicants. Size, budget, and media attention can indicate many things about an organization, like outreach capability and brand extension, but they don't guarantee that it is the best in its field. It's possible you'll find a smaller, humbler, less well-known organization serving its community or championing its cause more thoroughly and efficiently than the big guys, and the competition to join their staff may not be as fierce.

Keep in mind, too, that geography often determines the popularity of an issue. For example, if you live in the Pacific Northwest and are an environmentalist, you've got a lot of company—the environment is a hot topic in that part of the country, and many people will be competing with you to work in nonprofits devoted to environmentalism. The same goes for civil rights (such as same-sex marriage) in California, farming or agriculture in Wyoming, and immigration in Texas. But if you're willing to work on these hot-button issues in other parts of the country, you might be faced with less competition for the job of your choice, so long as you are willing to become intimately familiar with local issues. That means if you're going to seek out nonprofit work dealing with immigration in South Dakota, you'd better be ready to do your research and network like crazy to show you know a lot about South Dakota immigration issues and care specifically about immigrants in South Dakota. There may not be as much competition for immigration-related jobs, but what competition there is will be centered on a limited number of jobs, so be prepared to fight for them.

And if you are seeking work in a field that gets a lot of applicants, keep an open mind. Even though your main interest may be in coordinating cross-cultural events to raise public awareness of the issues immigrants face, don't ignore the posting for a position that entails helping immigrants acclimate to their new home. We're not suggesting you sacrifice your ambitions or go against what your self-assessment has revealed will be the best fit for you. We're just reminding you to keep your eyes open. Sometimes we pursue an option because it's the only one we know, but it's the unexpected opportunities that can provide the greatest adventures.

THE SEARCH—HOW IT LOOKS DIFFERENT

The more relevant experience you have, the more likely it is that you will be a front-runner when applying for a job. That's certainly true no matter what field you want to work in. But should you decide to pursue a career in the nonprofit world, you'll find that the avenues to gain that crucial experience are often wider and easier to come by than if you followed a more traditional career path.

For example, let's say you have spent fifteen years in a successful career in marketing. Though you're ready for a new challenge and know that you'd find greater fulfillment helping victims of child abuse, you have a mortgage and a family and other financial obligations that preclude your quitting your current job and starting over again with a non-marketing position at a nonprofit. But unlike the corporate world, in which unpaid internships and entry level positions are pretty much your only entry to a new field (with the exception of top executives, who are often hired for their management and business-building experience regardless of what field they started out in), in the nonprofit sphere you can gain relevant work experience without leaving your current employer. Besides the tried-and-true methods of working part-time or taking an internship, remember that there are other resources, such as time or expertise, that may help you get your foot in the door. You could:

Volunteer (General). This is an option for anyone, from the seasoned professional to the student, who wants to prove to a nonprofit that he is serious about committing himself to a particular issue. If you're interested in gaining experience with organizations that act on behalf of victims of child abuse, you might volunteer to help on a fund-raiser, or work on a nonprofit's newsletter, or even organize a local rally or community event. If you fit the requirements, you could take your volunteer efforts to another level by providing a foster home for a child or becoming a child advocate for the courts, also known as a *guardian ad litem*.

So what if you don't have an important title or can't put a big name on your resume? You can get a nonprofit's attention in other ways while you volunteer. Maybe you don't have fund-raising experience, but if you can get your current employer or your school or your neighborhood association to buy a table at a nonprofit's fund-raiser, you prove you are a serious advocate for the nonprofit's cause. You also reveal yourself as someone who can leverage important relationships on the nonprofit's behalf. Being known as a volunteer who can make things happen can lead to a greater profile within the organization, which can lead to an invitation to sit on the board, or even an invitation to join the staff.

Volunteer (Skilled). Skilled volunteerism is an excellent addition to a well-rounded resume, helping prospective nonprofit employers recognize the value of your for-profit experience. Someone with experience in marketing could find ample opportunities to use her skills on behalf of abused children. She could help a group draft and update their public relations material or their website. She could redesign the logo or act as a liaison between the organization and the media. Volunteering (skilled and general, though probably skilled to a greater extent) will also expose you to the unusual vocabulary used in nonprofits. (You can also go back and reread Chapter 2—it's a great primer for nonprofit terminology.) But not only will you be required to learn a new language, you'll also need to understand how a nonprofit is structured differently from the companies you may have worked for in the past. Volunteering, particularly at the higher levels accessible to a skilled volunteer, could give you the inside track should your organization decide that it needs someone working your position full-time. It will also give you a leg up on similarly skilled competition at other organizations, because potential supervisors might determine that you are less of a risk because you will require less hand-holding than someone completely new to the nonprofit world. Your work as a skilled volunteer will also equip you to convincingly explain in an interview how your professional skills can be successfully applied to the nonprofit's needs.

Become a Board Member. Individuals with marketing backgrounds, for example, can often be important additions to an organization's board. Such experience would offer someone interested in working full-time with a nonprofit an excellent opportunity to gain visibility in the nonprofit world, giving him the chance to show off his leadership abilities and reveal how he can apply the management, financial, and creative skills he garnered in his marketing career to the challenges particular to a nonprofit. This is true for other areas of expertise, as well. If you can get on the board of the nonprofit you're interested in working for, terrific. Such access to key players and inside information would give you a strong advantage when applying for a full-time position. Even if you can't get on the board of the specific organization you'd like to work for, board experience with any nonprofit that focuses on the same issue will still give you important insight into the needs of such an organization. You'll be able to take responsibility for an organization in a way that you rarely could in a for-profit without having put in years of service to the company.

Also, as in any field, people talk and mingle with their own It's likely that the people you meet on the board and through the nonprofit where you volunteer will have connections at other nonprofits in the community where you'd like to work. You can and should use that connection to your advantage once you're ready to activate your job search. That's right, you need to network.

NETWORKING

Some people are uncomfortable with the idea of using their relationships with others to their benefit, particularly in the nonprofit world, which many people want to believe is above the politics so prevalent in the corporate world. After all, in nonprofits it's about the mission, not the money, right? It's supposed to be about working together from a pure desire to help and a passion for a cause, not about jumping through hoops trying to prove you're better at your job than the next guy. Yet as we discussed in Chapter 10, nonprofits often have to play by the rules of good business if they are to accomplish their mission, which means that among other things they need to attract the best and brightest employees.

Now, many companies create a pool of candidates by sending recruiters to campuses around the country to promote their organization and cherry-pick the best candidates from those who express interest. For more senior positions, they may rely upon headhunters who can target accomplished professionals at other companies who might be open to a new job. Unfortunately, most nonprofits don't have the resources to hire recruiters, and it's unlikely that a marketing professional considering a switch to a nonprofit is going to hear from a headhunter. This means that if you want to hear about job openings, you're going to have to be extremely proactive. You can use the Internet, of course—Idealist .org has a constantly changing list of thousands of job opportunities available. The problem is that everyone else has access to that same list of jobs. Networking, however, will not only help you stand out from the faceless masses, it will also give you an inside track to job openings—the ones on the Internet and, perhaps more significantly, the ones that haven't been posted there yet or never will be. In addition, networking proves to organizations that you have an ability to connect with others, a highly desirable skill to nonprofits, since collaboration is often key to their success.

So don't be shy about reaching out to anyone who might have a link to the job you want—whether it's someone already working in the field, someone on your board, someone on the board of the nonprofit you're targeting, a friend, relative, professor, golf partner, or neighbor—and asking that person for help in the form of information, a reference, or a recommendation. But be careful how you ask for help. You may think there is only one job or one organization where you will be happy working, but it's in your best interest to keep your options open. You'll get more bites if you tell people, "I'm interested in working with an organization in the greater Boulder area related to animal welfare," as opposed to, "I want to work in a senior position at the Boulder Humane Society." You'll have a better chance at getting the job you actually want if you cast your net wide.

But I don't know anyone, you might say. This is hard to believe—everyone knows someone. And if that someone isn't the right someone, it's possible she knows someone who is. For example, let's say that you are currently a manager at Costco and are interested in a job at the local humane society but have no connection to that organization. You send out an email to your family and friends explaining your career ambitions and asking if they know anyone at the Humane Society you could speak to. You get no reply. Then your mother goes to the dentist for a routine checkup. There she mentions your aspirations, and the dentist reveals that her husband is a member of the board. You call the dentist, who refers you to her husband, who accepts your invitation for coffee and over a grande mocaccino gives you an in-depth explanation of how the organization works and what its needs will be in the future. You also take this opportunity to listen and ask informed questions. Next, you ask if your new contact could introduce you to the Humane Society's HR person or ED. Armed with an introduction from a board member, you're likely to get someone on staff to meet with you. Whether or not a job is currently available, you can still chat with him about future hires, how to strengthen your candidacy, and what other organizations he respects or knows are hiring.

If you don't want to wait around for a chance connection to strike, check out what opportunities you can find by networking through online communities. Try: Mid-Careers Transition Resource Center (www.idealist.org/en/midcareer) and Young Nonprofit Professionals Network (www.ynpn.org).

MAKING THE SWITCH

We met Antonio, Shannon, Molly, and Charles in Chapter 4 when they created self-assessment charts to pinpoint how their previous experiences and qualifications might lead them to a satisfying volunteer, board service, or philanthropic opportunity. But what happened next? Let's assume that they all got so much out of making their contributions that it inspired them to pursue careers in the nonprofit world. A glance at the distinct paths they took reveals how tapping into a combination of one's natural talents, life experience, professional skills, and social networks really is the key to creating a fulfilling career.

Growing up, Antonio loved playing video games, much to his mother's dismay. But in the end, that video game obsession became the springboard to a career that would make any mother proud. When we last met him, he was performing a self-assessment that pinpointed the experiences, interests, and qualifications that might serve him well if he were to volunteer with a nonprofit, serve on a board, or make a donation.

Antonio was never one to miss the newest electronic entertainment system, and had a closet full of old gaming equipment and video games to prove it. Rather than dump the wires, cables, game controllers, memory cards, every console ever invented, and several years' worth of Madden, Halo, and Final Fantasy, among others, he donated the entire collection to a nonprofit that provides gaming equipment to hospitals around the country for sick children to use. With no money or time to spare, he was elated to be able to improve a sick child's experience in the hospital in such a simple way.

After graduation, he found a job with an engineering firm that specialized in plastics, but even though he was no longer a student, he continued to feed his love for games with new ones and donated those he was done with. He rose up the corporate ladder to project manager before he was transferred to California, which happened to be the headquarters for the nonprofit that he had been supporting. He started volunteering, helping distribute and install systems at new hospitals. Eventually he realized that though he liked his job, he was happiest when working with the nonprofit and surrounded by other gamers all eager to bring a little joy into the lives of sick kids. His volunteer manager introduced him to the nonprofit's executive director, who was willing to sit down with him and discuss how the nonprofit might be able to use someone with his management and technical experience. It took several months, but eventually he was hired as partnerships manager, acting as a liaison between the nonprofit and companies interested in donating games, equipment, and money.

> I wanted to work for an organization doing work that I felt passionately about and that I felt would make a difference in people's lives. While I enjoyed my work in the for-profit sector, I didn't feel I was doing something unique, important, and making the world a better place. I got interested in women and development through volunteer activities, but I wanted to make a bigger contribution to the issues the nonprofit was addressing than I could have done while working at a for-profit full-time.
>
> —Betsy Werley, ED, The Transition Network

Shannon, as you'll recall, jumped off her career track to stay home with her children. Once the youngest started school, however, she sought out opportunities to get more involved with her community. She started spending a few mornings a week in the kitchen of a nonprofit that provided and distributed meals to homebound individuals with life-threatening illnesses. A talented baker, she added her cinnamon rolls to the breakfast menu. The rolls were such a hit that a local newspaper came to interview her, bringing much-needed public attention to the nonprofit and making Shannon one of the most popular volunteers there.

Eventually, she decided to go back to work part-time and, much to the nonprofit's disappointment, decided her schedule was too overloaded to volunteer anymore. She found, however, that she missed the camaraderie and community and sense of fulfillment she experienced at the nonprofit. The organization was small and had only six salaried positions, none of which was appropriate for her. The executive director, however, knew of a start-up nonprofit that needed a part-time Web design and layout consultant. Shannon interviewed with that organization's HR coordinator and the job was hers. She continued in this part-time position until her youngest started high school, at which time she pursued and easily won the position of director of communications.

Molly, an accountant with a love for modern dance, originally joined the board of a local dance company to add something interesting to her resume and expand her networking circle. Charged with donor outreach, however, she discovered that she had a knack for doing the hard sell with a soft touch, allowing her to build relationships with potential contributors and convince them that the dance company was a worthy recipient of their generosity. Thanks to her efforts, corporate and individual giving to the dance company grew by 40 percent over the two years she served on the board. The conclusion of her board term coincided with the departure of the development director, so the executive director, determined not to lose such an influential and effective force for the nonprofit, asked if Molly would consider joining the staff as development director, a position she happily accepted. After a year in the position, she realized that this work did not give her the same satisfaction she had experienced as a member of the board. Though as development director she doubled the size of the organization's donor base, she was frustrated by the day-to-day pressures and the lack of involvement she had with programs. So she made another switch. She now works as a financial consultant for local arts nonprofits and serves on several local boards where she can again enjoy the challenge of fund-raising.

Newly retired Charles thought he would love having so much free time. For the first time in forty years, he had time to read, time to play with his band, time to travel, time to fly kites with the grandkids. In the beginning the life of leisure felt great, but after six months all that free time was starting to drive Charles crazy. He wasn't relaxed, and he wasn't happy. He missed feeling that he was contributing something to society, and decided to find a way to infuse meaning back into his life. He found it by volunteering at a nonprofit dedicated to supporting individuals with cognitive and developmental disabilities. Though a pharmacist by profession, he was also a talented musician, so he started offering group music and rhythm classes twice a week. The response was so great he eventually had to start teaching a few hours every day to keep up with demand. Inspired by the immediate good he could do for the people who sought him out, he enrolled at the local university to pursue a degree in music therapy. He now works as a part-time music therapist at various nonprofits throughout the city, a schedule that also allows him plenty of time to fly kites with the grandkids.

STAY TRUE TO YOUR PASSION

When working for a nonprofit, the mission has to matter. If you've been a career salesperson, it's possible that in one job you sold cars and in another you sold copiers. While enthusiasm for your product was always important, the art of the sale was probably more critical to performing your job well than mustering up a passion for cars or copiers, making it feasible to easily transfer your skills from one job to the next. But if you're switching to a nonprofit career from another career, or even after time away from a career, the skills you transfer to the nonprofit, while important to your success in the position, should be matched by the passion you feel for the nonprofit's cause. Had Charles been interested in earning extra cash, he could have taught private music lessons. Had he simply wanted to pass the time, he could have offered piano concerts at a local senior citizen's home. But Charles excelled as a volunteer because the nonprofit's mission allowed him to provide the best of what he had to offer—a passion for helping people through music—and gave him the sense of fulfillment and achievement he was looking for.

By the way, just by virtue of being a nonprofit an organization will not necessarily provide you with a more satisfactory working experience than the corporate world might. Indeed, many of the negatives one associates with working in the for-profit sector also exist within nonprofits. Remember how we encouraged you at the end of Chapter 1 to get to know yourself by asking you to think about what matters to you and how to get the most out of your contribution of time, money, or expertise to a nonprofit? And how in Chapter 3 we asked you to consider, among other things, your purpose, your ambition, and whether you prefer direct or indirect contact? This is where that self-assessment will help you stay on the right track. If you've already established that you need immediate gratification in order to feel that your work has had an impact, you'll have a better chance at professional happiness if you pursue the job that puts you on the front lines with the clients a nonprofit serves, rather than the administrative one, even if the administrative job offers better pay. After all, if you accept the better-paying job only to quit six months later in disappointment, what will you have accomplished? Stay true to yourself and your passion, and you'll get what you want—a fulfilling career centered around making someone's world, maybe even your own, a better place.

IDEALISM IN ACTION

I LEFT [MY PREVIOUS GOVERNMENT JOB] BECAUSE OF A LEADERSHIP TRANSITION, BUT I WAS ALSO SEEKING A WAY TO WORK ON THE SAME SORTS OF ISSUES CONCERNING CHILDREN AND FAMILIES IN A MORE FLEXIBLE, LESS BUREAUCRATIC ENVIRONMENT—AND ONE THAT WAS LESS POLITICIZED. I FOUND A BETTER MATCH FOR MY INTERESTS AND TALENTS IN THE NONPROFIT SECTOR . . . I LOVE WORKING FOR A MISSION THAT I AM PASSIONATE ABOUT, AND BEING SURROUNDED BY PEOPLE WHO CARE DEEPLY ABOUT TRYING TO MAKE THE WORLD A BETTER PLACE. I LOVE THE OPTIMISM THAT PEOPLE MAINTAIN, EVEN IN THE FACE OF MANY CHALLENGES.

—Chris Tebben, executive director, Grantmakers for Education

Conclusion

Actions Speak Louder Than Words

When it comes to making a contribution, financial or otherwise, actions really do speak louder than words. It's commendable to talk about "getting involved" or "making a difference," but you're not doing anyone any good until you actually turn that intention into action. So are you ready to get off that hamster wheel of routine? Are you ready to live a life in which giving is as natural and necessary as breathing? Do you see ways in which you can use your professional skills and resources to increase your impact on the community? Isn't it inspiring to know how little it can take to make an enormous difference? We hope so, not just because we are eager to see you join the ranks of idealists doing what they can to make the world a better place, but because it's been proven over and over again that people who give are people who are happy; indeed, they are significantly happier than people who don't give. This holds true across the board, whether we analyze rates of philanthropy or volunteerism or informal giving such as blood donations or buying a homeless person a cup of coffee. According to the Social Capital Benchmark Survey in 2000, people who give money to charity are 43 percent more likely than people who don't donate money to say they are happy. And people who volunteer are 42 percent more likely to say they are happy than people who don't. These results are consistent regardless of where people fall on the financial, social, professional, or religious spectrum.[10] Another survey conducted from 1988 to 2006 by the University of Chicago revealed that the happiest American workers are those who work in professions that serve others.

Why? What is it about giving that seems to make people happy, even those who might be financially or socially disadvantaged? Some researchers say it's because the act of giving enhances the way we see ourselves and the way we think others perceive us. Others think it has to do with the often unexpected reciprocal giving we get in the form of a thank-you or a smile. And some suggest that while we get a surge of happiness when we buy something we desperately want, like a new car, we eventually get used to that possession, whereas the act of giving taps into a bottomless tank of good feelings that we can revisit over and over. Regardless, it's clear that giving is more than just a good thing to do; it's actually good for you. In the words of Aristotle, "Happiness is a state of activity." Think about that on your first day as a volunteer, or the first time you make that donation, or the first time you sit on a board, or the day you accept a job offer from your dream nonprofit.

Our intent was to write a book that went beyond a cut-and-dried explanation of how nonprofits work and what options they might afford you to do good. The world has enough of those, thank you. And as you discovered, there is very little that is cut-and-dried about nonprofits anyway. Their world is a dynamic, fluid, complex one, populated by idealists whose backgrounds, experience, and motives defy labels and categorization. Theirs is a club in which membership hinges on only one common thread: they saw a problem that needed to be solved, a group that needed some support, an issue that deserved attention, and they did something about it.

You can join that club. You, too, can build a better world by volunteering, or donating money, or sharing your expertise. You can make it your life's work, or simply part of your life. You have all the tools you need to get started. There are countless ways to make a difference, and we hope that we've led you toward one, or several, that will give you a boundless sense of personal satisfaction. Ultimately, you'll find that you've not only enriched the individual or community or cause that benefited from your efforts, but enriched your own life as well, for when you turn your good intentions into action, you plant the seeds for change, and the seeds of your own legacy.

Appendix A

Nine Types of Nonprofits

In Chapter 2 we promised you a comprehensive list of the types of nonprofits that make up the approximately 1.4 million organizations that operate in the United States. The easiest way to get an idea of the variety of nonprofits out there is through the NTEE system (National Taxonomy of Exempt Entities), which the IRS uses for statistical purposes. It classifies nonprofits into nine categories, plus the catchall "Unknown" for groups that haven't been classified yet. These categories are pretty broad, though, so to help you recognize why a nonprofit might be considered an educational nonprofit instead of one devoted to human services, for example, we're going to delve deeper into what these labels really mean. Many nonprofits don't fit neatly into one box. We've provided a random sampling of examples so you can see for yourself the rich variety of nonprofits that exist within every category. It's an interesting list. After all, while you'd certainly expect to see organizations that address the needs of the homeless or the environment, it might surprise you to learn that there is a nonprofit devoted to promoting handbell and handchime music, another dedicated to knee research, and still another to rock 'n' roll music. There is a nonprofit out there for almost everybody.[11]

1. Arts, culture, and humanities

These are the organizations that enrich our lives by promoting and educating us about the visual, performing, folk, and media arts; communications, including film, TV, publishing, and radio, and museums (including children's and science museums). That's to be expected. But this category also includes agencies that work toward an appreciation of modern and classical languages, ethics, comparative religion, theology, cultural and ethnic awareness, community celebrations, and historical societies and historic preservation.

Examples:

Parents Television Council, Inc.; Colorado Alliance for Arts Education, Inc.; Metropolitan Museum of Art; Society of Illustrators, Inc.; American Guild of English Handbell Ringers, Inc.; Association for Computational Linguistics; Nigerian American Public Professionals Association; Oregon Shakespeare Festival; Up With People; Kansas City Men's Choir

2. Education

Here, too, the categorization is pretty self-explanatory. It includes preschools and elementary and secondary schools (including Montessoris, boarding schools, and yeshivas), vocational schools, colleges and universities, libraries, ESL programs, literacy programs, scholarship programs, and education-related services such as drop-out prevention agencies. It also happens to include sororities and fraternities, alumni organizations, and parent/teacher groups.

Examples:

Cornell University, Palm Springs High School Instrumental Band Boosters, Reading Is Fundamental, John F. Kennedy Presidential Library and Museum, César Chávez Public Charter Schools for Public Policy, Beta Theta Pi Fraternity Parent Teacher Association, American Educational Research Association, Hispanic Scholarship Fund

3. Environment and animals

Any organization whose primary purpose is to improve and protect the environment, and/or care for, protect, and control wildlife and domestic pets will fall under this category. Environmental groups that fall under this label are anti-pollution organizations; recycling advocates; water, land, energy, and forest conservation groups; park beautification groups; even botanical gardens. Groups promoting animal welfare, as well as humane societies and some veterinary services, zoos, and wildlife sanctuaries, also qualify.

Examples:

Nature Conservancy; National Audubon Society, Inc.; New York Botanical Garden; PEDAL; California Releaf;

Humane Society of the United States; Neighborhood Cats, Inc.; San Diego Zoo; Tennessee Aquarium; Elephant Sanctuary; Humane Farming Association; Ducks Unlimited

4. Health

A large number of nonprofits will wind up under the health category. Some obvious suspects would be hospitals, clinics; family planning centers; rehabilitation centers; home health care agencies; and blood, organ, and tissue banks. Facilities that treat mental health patients are also categorized here, including substance abuse programs and crisis hotlines. Agencies that work to prevent specific diseases, such as Down's Syndrome or cancer, will also be included, as well as most research organizations dedicated to specific illnesses.

Examples:

American Cancer Society; Mayo Foundation; Dauphin Middle Paxton Community Ambulance Association; Alcoholics Anonymous; Latin Physicians Network Foundation; Women's Collective; Asthma Athletics; Los Angeles Intergroup of Overeaters Anonymous, Inc.; Michael J. Fox Foundation for Parkinson Research; La Leche League International; National Knee Research and Education Foundation, Inc.; American Association of Poison Control Centers

5. Human services

Human services is another enormous catchall category. It refers to groups that provide any of a broad range of social services for individuals and families. This label also applies to organizations that address crime- and legal-related issues, including drunk driving prevention programs and halfway houses; employment, including professional associations; food, agriculture, and nutrition; housing and shelter, which not only includes homeless shelters but also organizations that build or manage housing for low-income residents, senior citizens, or the disabled; public safety; disaster preparedness and relief; recreation and sports, including camps, rec centers, and parks and playgrounds; and finally, youth development, including youth centers and Scouts.

Examples:

Dress for Success; Pro Bono Net, Inc.; Cabrini Green Legal Aid Clinic; Farm Aid, Inc.; Slow Food; Habitat for Humanity; Boat People SOS; Sojourner Project, Inc.; Stop Prisoner Rape; Goodwill Industries; AFL-CIO Appalachian Council, Inc.; Father Flanagan's Boys Home; Houston Volunteer Fire Company; United States Golf Association; Elderhostel, Inc.; Boy Scouts of America; Young Life; American National Red Cross; Children's Aid Society; Jewish Family Services; Helping Hand Rescue Mission; America's Second Harvest; Central Park Conservancy

6. International, foreign affairs, and national security

If you've ever hosted a foreign exchange student, you probably did it through an organization that falls under this classification. Not only does the label include organizations that focus on economic development, human rights, arms control, and other national security issues, but it also includes cultural exchange groups like traveling theater troupes.

Examples:

AFS Intercultural Programs; International Rescue Committee; Human Rights Watch; Catholic Network of Volunteer Service; International Justice Mission; Vaccine Fund; International Foreign Exchange Program; Feed the Children, Inc.; Institute for Trade and Commercial Diplomacy; National Defense Council, Inc.

7. Public, societal benefit

This is the second-largest category, encompassing organizations that focus on improving governmental oversight, functions, agencies, and community involvement and awareness of these issues; agencies that promote and protect individual and group rights (the disabled, minorities, women, right to life, etc.); community improvement and capacity building, such as economic development groups and neighborhood associations; philanthropy, voluntarism, and grant-making foundations (any group dedicated to promoting philanthropic and volunteer activities or providing funds for the benefit of nonprofit agencies); organizations dedicated to researching, promoting, and educating the public about science and technology; social science (anthropology, urban studies, etc.) research; and educational organizations.

Examples:

Points of Light; La Raza; National Disability Rights Network; North Carolina Association of Community Development Corporations; Children's Defense Fund; Maryland Right to Life Foundation; Catholics for a Free Choice; Self-Help Ventures Fund; High Point Community Pride Association; Jewish Communal Fund; Institute of Electrical and Electronics Engineers, Inc.; Maryland Space Business Roundtable, Inc.; Pilot Career Foundation; First Robot, Inc.; American Psychological Association, Inc.; American Dialect Society; Highland County Veterans Honor Guard; Citizens Against Government Waste; Korean American League for Civic Action, Inc.

8. Religion related

Churches, synagogues, mosques, temples, and other places of worship are probably the first things that spring to mind when we think about a religious nonprofit. But aside from these religious institutions are thousands of faith-based nonprofits working on issues that range beyond the immediate needs of a congregation. In addition, this category includes religious media, such as radio, TV, film, and publishing.

Examples:

Billy Graham Evangelistic Association; Jewish Vocational Services; Christian Broadcasting Network; American Bible Society; Eritrean Orthodox Church of St. Mary in Chicago; Mission Printing, Inc.; La Paloma Ministries, Inc., Knoxville Jewish Alliance; Muslims on Long Island, Inc., Quang Chieu Buddhist Meditation Association; Sri Annamacharya Project of North America, Inc.; Institute of Interfaith Dialogue; Lutheran Community Services

9. Mutual/Membership benefit

Any agency formed to insure or benefit the members of a particular group would fall under this category, like pension and retirement funds, workers' comp, benevolent life insurance associations, fraternal societies, and cemeteries. Yes, cemeteries.

Examples:

International Workers' Compensation Foundation, Inc.; Freemasons; Grand Forks Fastbreak Club, Inc.; Ancient Mystical Order of Rosae Crucis; Tucson Scottish Rite Cathedral Foundation, Inc.; Elks Club; Thrivant Financial for Lutherans

Appendix B

Additional Resources on Idealist.org

RESOURCES FOR LOCAL ACTION

Do you have a great idea to improve your community and need a little help getting started? Idealist.org offers a number of tools and resources to help you get your project off the ground.

Idealist's **Community Action Center** (www.idealist.org/cac) is a free resource center that can help you plan and sustain a project to make your community a better place. Full of tips and tools on topics like fund-raising, leadership, and working with the media, the CAC covers the key aspects of running a community action project and is also available in French and Spanish. If you're an up-and-coming world changer, **Generation Idealist** (www.idealist.org/generation idealist) is for you. This resource center is dedicated to students and young people who want to have an impact on their community.

VOLUNTEERING RESOURCES

Our **Volunteer Resource Center** (www.idealist.org/volunteer) and **International Volunteerism Resource Center** (www.idealist .org/ivrc) offer a wealth of advice to help you learn about and find great volunteer experiences in your community or around the world. Combined with Idealist's fifteen thousand worldwide volunteer listings, these resource centers create a one-stop shop for would-be volunteers.

Idealist **Global Volunteering Fairs** (www.idealist.org/global volunteering) take place around the United States. These events bring together leading volunteer-sending organizations and people inter- ested in exploring the array of international service opportunities, from short volunteer vacations to longer service programs. The fairs also feature panel discussions on topics like whether to go abroad on your own or through a program and how to decide where to go and what to do.

NONPROFIT JOBS AND CAREERS

With more than eight thousand nonprofit jobs posted on the site, one of the easiest ways to kick-start your search for work with meaning is to create a free profile on Idealist.org. Once you've registered, you can receive customized, **free email alerts** about available positions (paid and volunteer), events, and other resources in your area or any- where else.

Visit the Idealist **Career Center** (www.idealist.org/career) for useful career advice and job-search strategies. From salary surveys to career profiles, the Career Center is one of the Web's largest sources of information about nonprofit careers.

The **Idealist Guides to Nonprofit Careers** are two free, comprehensive books about how to find meaningful work in the nonprofit sector—one for first-time job seekers and another for mid-career professionals. Full of practical advice, reflective exercises, revealing statistics, and ideas for structuring your job search, both editions are available for download as PDFs at www.idealist.org/careerguide.

If your career path isn't following a straight line like you thought it would, you're not alone! Idealist's **Mid-Career Transitions Resource Center** (www.idealist.org/mctrc) offers targeted information and guidance for people in a variety of situations who are considering a change in career directions toward nonprofit work.

Idealist recognizes that a valuable entry point to public service careers is participating in a term of service. Our **Term-of-Service Resource Center** (www.idealist.org/tos) aims to educate people about the range of service options, and creates events and resources to support participants when they complete their term of service.

Held in cities across the United States, Idealist **Nonprofit Career Fairs** (www.idealist.org/careerfairs) bring together job seekers and local, national, and international nonprofit organizations offering jobs, internships, and volunteer opportunities. These fairs (free for job seekers) also feature informative panels to help you understand the sector and build job-search skills.

IF YOU ARE THINKING ABOUT GRADUATE SCHOOL

If you're considering graduate school as part of your path to a social change career, Idealist also has resources and events for you. Our **Public Service Graduate Education Resource Center** (www.ideal ist.org/psgerc) features informative articles and advice for anyone looking to connect their graduate education options with their future work in the social sector.

Idealist Graduate Degree Fairs for the Public Good (www .idealist.org/gradfairs), held in cities around the United States and in other countries, are free events that give you a chance to meet representatives from a range of graduate programs focused on helping their students prepare to make a difference in the world. The fairs also feature panel discussions on topics like which degree is right for you, the admissions process, and financial aid options.

FOR NONPROFIT PROFESSIONALS

If you're a nonprofit professional, Idealist.org offers many tools to help you improve your work and expand your knowledge. By creating a profile on Idealist, you can **post a range of information** about your organization—from events, resources, and campaigns to internships and volunteer positions and jobs.

Idealist also runs specialized resource centers on nonprofit topics. The **Nonprofit FAQ** (www.idealist.org/npofaq) features a huge selection of Q&As about important nonprofit management themes, from advocacy and fund-raising to board-staff relations and leadership.

The Idealist **Nonprofit HR Resource Center** (www.idealist .org/nonprofithr) collects useful information on all aspects of HR from a nonprofit perspective. With focus areas like recruiting, compensation and benefits, employee development, and retention, this resource center can help you, whether you're an "HR department of one" or part of a team of managers at an organization undergoing rapid growth.

Our **Volunteer Management Resource Center** (www.idealist .org/vmrc) helps volunteer managers develop programs to create and sustain truly meaningful and organizationally valuable volunteer engagement. And with its career profiles, statistics, and position descriptions, the Volunteer Management Resource Center can also serve as a gateway to a career in volunteer management.

Additional Reading

Along with the websites listed in each chapter, the following books and resources were useful in the writing of this book.

Benioff, Marc, and Carlye Adler. *The Business of Changing the World: Twenty Great Leaders on Strategic Corporate Philanthropy.* New York: McGraw Hill, 2007.

BoardSource, www.boardsource.org.

Brooks, Arthur. *Gross National Happiness: Why Happiness Matters for America and How We Can Get More of It.* New York: Basic Books, 2008.

Brown, Howard H., and Donald L. Ruhl. *Breakthrough Management for Not-for-Profit Organizations: Beyond Survival in the 21st Century.* Westport, CT: Praeger Publishers, 2003.

Foundation Center, www.foundationcenter.org.

Freedman, Marc. *Encore: Finding Work That Matters in the Second Half of Life.* New York: Public Affairs, 2008.

Friedman, Milton. *Capitalism and Freedom,* 40th Anniversary Edition. Chicago: University of Chicago Press, 2002.

Gary, Tracy, and Melissa Kohner. *Inspired Philanthropy: Creating a Giving Plan*. Berkeley, CA: Chardon Press, 1998.

Guidestar, www.guidestar.org.

Hollender, Jeffrey, with Stephen Fenichell. *What Matters Most: How a Small Group of Pioneers Is Teaching Social Responsibility to Big Business, and Why Big Business Is Listening*. New York: Basic Books, 2004.

Internal Revenue Service, www.irs.gov.

Karlgaard, Rich. *Life 2.0: How People Across America Are Transforming Their Lives by Finding the Where of Their Happiness*. New York: Three Rivers Press, 2004.

Mancuso, Anthony. *How to Form a Nonprofit Corporation in All 50 States*. Berkeley, CA: Nolo Press, 1997.

National Center for Charitable Statistics, www.nccs.urban.org.

Newman Ed.D., Raquel. *Giving Away Your Money: A Personal Guide to Philanthropy*. Rockville, MD: Schreiber Publishing, 2000.

Nicholas, Ted. *The Complete Guide to Nonprofit Corporations: Step-by-Step Guidelines and Procedures and Forms to Maintain a Nonprofit Company*. Chicago: Dearborn Financial Publishing, 1993.

O'Neill, Michael. *Nonprofit Nation: A New Look at the Third America*. San Francisco: Jossey-Bass, 2002.

Salamon, Lester M. *America's Nonprofit Sector: A Primer*, 2nd Edition. New York: The Foundation Center, 1999.

Tax History Museum, www.tax.org/museum/default.htm.

Endnotes

1. *Wall Street Journal Online*, Personal Finance Poll, vol. 2, issue 10, December 28, 2006, www.harrisinteractive.com/news/newsletters/WSJfinance//HI_WSJ_PersFinPoll_2006_vol2_iss10.pdf.
2. Ibid.
3. Salamon, *America's Nonprofit Sector*, 10.
4. National Center for Charitable Statistics, www.nccs.urban.org/resources/faq.cfm.
5. "2007 Report on Socially Responsible Investing Trends in the United States," Social Investment Forum, www.socialinvest.org/pdf/SRI_Trends_ExecSummary_2007.pdf.
6. Social Funds, www.socialfunds.com/news/article.cgi/article832.html.
7. Friedman, *Capitalism and Freedom*, 133.
8. Social Funds, www.socialfunds.com/news/article.cgi/article832.html.

9. Orlitzky, Mark, Frank L. Schmidt, and Sara L. Rynes, "Corporate Social and Financial Performance: A Meta-Analysis," *Organization Studies* 24, no. 3 (2003): 403–441.

10. Brooks, *Gross National Happiness*, 176–177.

11. For an even more detailed breakdown and explanation of all NTEE codes, go to the National Center for Charitable Statistics Data Web (http://nccsdataweb.urban.org).

Index